THE VIETNAM WAR

VIRGINIA SCHOMP

Benchmark Books

MARSHALL CAVENDISH
NEW YORK

Benchmark Books
Marshall Cavendish Corporation
99 White Plains Road
Tarrytown, New York 10591-9001
Website: www.marshallcavendish.com

Library of Congress Cataloging-in-Publication Data
Schomp, Virginia.
The Vietnam War / by Virginia Schomp.
p. cm. – (Letters from the homefront)
Includes bibliographical references and index.
ISBN 0-7614-1099-6 (lib. bdg.)
1. Vietnamese Conflict, 1961-1975—United States—Juvenile literature. 2. United States—Politics and government—1945-1989—Juvenile literature. [1. Vietnamese Conflict, 1961–1975. 2. United States—Social conditions—1960-1980. 3. Letters.] I. Title. II. Series.
DS558 .S36 2001 959.704'3373—dc21 00-046770

Book design by Carol Matsuyama
Photo Research by Anne Burns Images
Printed in Italy
6 5 4 3 2 1

Photo Credits
Cover by: UPI/Corbis-Bettman
All photographs in this book are used by permission and through the courtesy of: *Bridgeman Art Library*: 9. *John F. Kennedy Library*: 13. *Corbis*: UPI Bettman: 15, 23, 27, 28, 37, 38, 39, 41 (l&r), 42, 43, 50, 53, 54, 57, 71, 79, 81; Tim Page: 48; Wally McNamee: 67; James Blair: 77. *National Archives*: 20. *Archive Photos*: 31, 36; Joseph Sia: 63; Michael Evans/NY Times: 69; Leif Skoogfors: 70. *LBJ Library*: Yoichi Okamoto: 35. *SuperStock*: 66; Xavier Jones: 45, 47. *TimePix*: Arthur Schatz: 61.

ACKNOWLEDGMENTS

With thanks to Glenn C. Altschuler, the Thomas and Dorothy Litwin Professor of American Studies, Cornell University, Ithaca, New York, for his expert reading of the manuscript.

Every effort has been made to trace the copyright holders of letters and other personal writings used in this book. We apologize for any omissions or errors in this regard and would be pleased to make the appropriate acknowledgment in any future printings.
      Grateful acknowledgments are made to the following individuals, organizations, and publishers:

Bobbie Lou Pendergrass to John F. Kennedy, February 18, 1963. White House Central Subject File, Box 604, John Fitzgerald Kennedy Library, Boston, MA. Courtesy of the National Archives and Records Administration.

William Ehrhart oral history appears by courtesy of W. D. Ehrhart.

Bill Clinton to Lt. Col. Eugene Holmes, December 3, 1969. From *Citizen's Reform Forum* at http://www.phonet.com/~bsimon/wjcdraft.htm and *Bill Clinton's Christmas Letter* at http://www.olywa.net/sdotctho/bhl1.htm

Rita to Dennis Giunta, April 7, 1967. Courtesy of Dennis Giunta.

Jeff Schomp to the Livingston, New Jersey, *West Essex Tribune*, June 5, 1969. Author's personal collection.

Dr. Martin Luther King, Jr., "Letter from Birmingham Jail," April 16, 1963. Reprinted by arrangement with the estate of Martin Luther King, Jr., care of Writers House as agent for the proprietor. Copyright © 1963 Martin Luther King, Jr.. Copyright renewed 1991 Coretta Scott King.

Malcolm X telegram to Dr. Martin Luther King., Jr., June 30, 1964. From *Malcolm X: A Research Site*, edited by Abdul Alkalimat, at http://www.brothermalcolm.net; as reproduced from Emerge magazine, February 1998.

"Mel" oral history from *Watts: The Aftermath, An Inside View of the Ghetto*, edited by Paul Bullock, published by Grove/Atlantic, Inc., copyright 1969.

Letter to Betty Friedan, copyright ©1963, 1964, 1966, 1970, 1971, 1972, 1973, 1974, 1975, 1976, 1985, 1991, 1998 by Betty Friedan. First appeared in *It Changed My Life*, published by Random House, currently published by Harvard University Press. Reprinted by permission of Curtis Brown, Ltd.

Anne Simon Auger oral history. Reprinted with permission from *A Piece of My Heart* by Keith Walker ©1985, Presidio Press, Novato, CA 94945.

Helen Hightower to Gary Kellerman, November 22, 1993. Courtesy of the New Jersey Vietnam Veterans' Memorial and Vietnam Era Educational Center. Reprinted by permission of Gary Kellerman.

Letter from Gregory Olsen to "Dad" (Samuel G. Olsen), March 14, 1968. From *My Lai 4: A Report on the Massacre and Its Aftermath* by Seymour M. Hersh, published by Random House, 1970. Reprinted by permission of Seymour M. Hersh.

Watergate transcript, June 23, 1972. From *History and Politics Out Loud* at http://database.library.northwestern.edu/hpol/transcript.asp?id=92 and *The Final Days*, by Bob Woodward and Carl Bernstein, published by Simon and Schuster, 1976.

Three letters left at the Vietnam Veterans Memorial. From *Shrapnel in the Heart: Letters and Remembrances from the Vietnam Veterans Memorial* by Laura Palmer, ©1987 by Laura Palmer, Random House. Reprinted courtesy of Random House.

Sincere thanks are also extended to Katie Jones at the New Jersey Vietnam Veterans' Memorial and Vietnam Era Educational Center; to the ever-helpful librarians and staff at the E. B. Crawford Library, Monticello, New York; and to the many "internet pals" who helped with research and outreach to Vietnam veterans and their families, including Linda ("Texastwister"), Dennis Hodo, Dennis Giunta, Larry Skoglund, Jim Willingham, Don Coffman of AMVETS, Ann Crawford of Military Living Publications, BJ of the Marine Corps Wives website, Dina of the Children of Vietnam Vets website, Robert Wheatley of the TLC Brotherhood, Walter Rice of VETS4EVER, and Joe Miller of VVAW.

In memory of
Jeffrey T. Schomp
(1946–1971)

and in honor of all those who served,
and all who waited for their return

CONTENTS

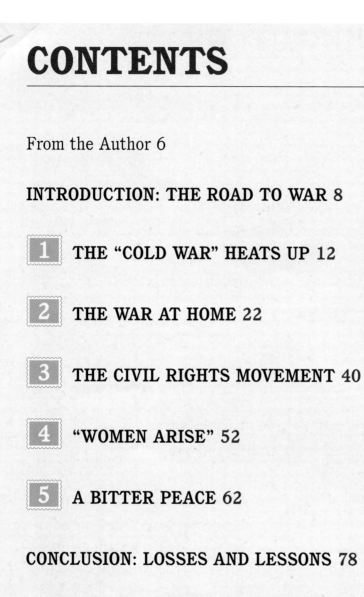

FROM THE AUTHOR

The Letters from the Homefront series got its start in my mother's attic. While rummaging through an old packing trunk stored there, I came across a box of letters written by my oldest brother in 1970–1971, when he served in the army during the Vietnam War. Further searching uncovered a treasure trove of even older family letters, some tucked in shoe boxes, some stacked in tidy bundles tied with faded ribbons. There were notes written by my future grandmother on the eve of World War I and letters from my father describing the B-29 Superfortress bomber he trained in as a tail gunner during World War II. There were cartons filled with fascinating keepsakes: postcards, photographs, a food ration book, dusty magazines and record albums, the star banner my mother hung in her front window nearly sixty years ago to show that she had a husband in the service. Each of these items tells a story. Together they offer not only a glimpse into my own family's past but also a snapshot of American life and culture during various times in our nation's history.

Historians often study letters and journals written by famous people—explorers, philosophers, presidents, kings—to gain information about the past. Recently they have discovered the value of writings by "ordinary" people, too. Students of history have begun to seek out and study the personal writings of homemakers, merchants, teachers, farmers, and foot soldiers. Documents like these—often called primary sources—bring a personal voice to history, helping us to understand how earlier generations lived, worked, and played, and how historical events shaped their lives.

This book employs primary sources to explore life in America during the Vietnam War. In these pages you will hear the voices of both "hawks" and "doves"—those who supported American involvement in Vietnam and those who bitterly opposed it. You will meet "baby boomers" inspired by President John F. Kennedy's call to public service and radicals intent on overthrowing the U.S. government. You will experience the anger and frustration of African Americans fighting for their civil rights and women struggling for full equality. Through the letters and remembrances of those who lived through the Vietnam War years, you will share the energy, excitement, triumphs, and tragedies of an era that brought dramatic change to nearly every aspect of life on the American homefront.

INTRODUCTION: THE ROAD TO WAR

U.S. involvement in Vietnam did not begin with a hail of bullets or rocket fire, a call to arms or patriotic speeches. Instead, America crept into its longest and most controversial war slowly, one small step at a time, like a hiker wading aimlessly into quicksand.

Before most Americans had ever heard of Vietnam, this small country in the southeastern corner of Asia already had a long history. Since ancient times the Vietnamese people had struggled against a series of foreign conquerors, battling again and again to win their independence. France seized control in the mid-1800s. As a French colony, Vietnam saw its natural resources stripped, its people cheated out of their land and mistreated. Finally a new leader emerged in the Vietnamese fight for freedom—the fiery revolutionary Ho Chi Minh (hoe-chee-MIN).

In 1945 Ho declared Vietnam independent from France. He asked the United States to support his cause, but government leaders refused. World War II had just ended, and Americans were worried about the growing power of the Soviet Union, a former ally that seemed intent on spreading Communism throughout the world. Ho Chi Minh was a Communist. To U.S. leaders, that made him an enemy. Later, in 1950, America sent money and a few military advisers to help the French defeat Vietnam's Communist forces.

The French were well trained and well armed. But the Vietnamese were fighting on familiar ground, in defense of their homes and their freedom. They waged a hit-and-run "guerrilla" war, ambushing French troops, damaging roads and bridges, then vanishing like ghosts into the forests and mountains. By 1954 Ho's

tiến lên
toàn thắng
ắt về ta

HO CHI MINH LED NORTH VIETNAM'S FIGHT AGAINST THE U.S.-SUPPORTED GOVERNMENT OF SOUTH VIETNAM. THE SLOGAN ON THIS 1960 VIETNAMESE POSTER READS, "ADVANCE, VICTORY IS OURS."

guerrillas had brought France to its knees. After a crushing defeat in the Battle of Dien Bien Phu (dyen-byen-FOO), the French army pulled out of Vietnam. Under agreements reached at a peace conference in Geneva, Switzerland, the country was divided in two. The northern half, with its capital at Hanoi, would be ruled by Ho Chi Minh. In the south President Ngo Dinh Diem (no-din-zee-EM) headed a rival government at Saigon.

The U.S. supported Diem. Beginning in 1955, under President Dwight Eisenhower, hundreds of American military advisers were sent to South Vietnam to help train its army. Millions of U.S. dollars poured into Diem's anti-Communist government. Many South Vietnamese hated the Communists, who ruled like dictators in the

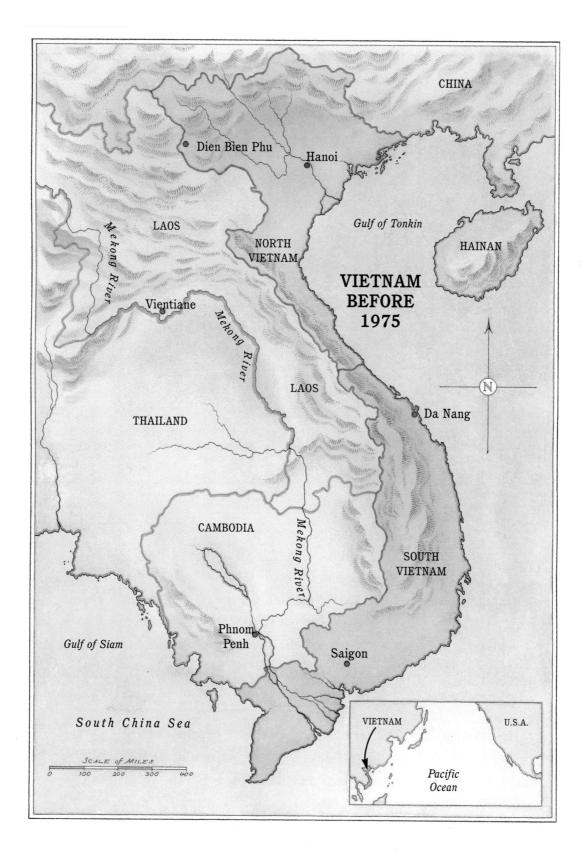

CHINA

Dien Bien Phu

Hanoi

Gulf of Tonkin

LAOS

Mekong River

NORTH
VIETNAM

**VIETNAM
BEFORE
1975**

HAINAN

Vientiane

Mekong River

THAILAND

LAOS

N

Da Nang

CAMBODIA

Mekong River

SOUTH
VIETNAM

Phnom
Penh

Saigon

Gulf of Siam

South China Sea

SCALE of MILES

0   100   200   300   400

VIETNAM

U.S.A.

*Pacific
Ocean*

north, brutally punishing all who objected to their strict policies. There were also many people, both north and south, who saw Ho Chi Minh as a hero and patriot. These Vietnamese Communists gained support as President Diem set up his own harsh dictatorship, appointing dishonest officials who robbed and terrorized South Vietnamese villagers.

By 1960 North and South Vietnam were in an all-out civil war. Ho Chi Minh's guerrillas controlled most of the countryside, and it looked as if President Diem's government was near an end. But the "problem" of Vietnam was about to be turned over to a new American president, a young man who pledged to "bear any burden" in support of democracy. President John F. Kennedy would take the United States a few critical steps deeper into the quicksand of the Vietnam War.

THE "COLD WAR" HEATS UP

The idealism of JFK had a profound [very deep] effect on our generation. When he declared a torch had been passed to a new generation of Americans, we assumed he meant us. . . . In following Kennedy's vision we believed we could serve the nation and the truth. All things seemed possible.

—DAVID OBST, A CALIFORNIA "BABY BOOMER"

Taking a Stand

He was handsome, elegant, and young—the youngest man ever elected to the presidency. And when John F. Kennedy took office in 1961, millions of young Americans enthusiastically embraced him as *their* president. These young people belonged to the "baby boom" generation. They had been born in record numbers in the peaceful, prosperous years following World War II. Raised in a time of rising incomes and expectations, they were proud and optimistic, ready and willing to take on new challenges. President Kennedy tapped into their idealism—their eager belief that they could change the world. When he asked Americans to help him "assure a more fruitful life for all mankind," thousands answered the call, joining the newly formed Peace Corps to help needy people in foreign countries and volunteering for service work in their own communities.

THE YOUNGEST MAN EVER ELECTED PRESIDENT, JOHN F. KENNEDY CALLED ON AMERICANS TO LIVE UP TO THE HARD WORK AND SACRIFICES OF EARLIER GENERATIONS.

The Torch Is Passed

A gifted and inspiring speaker, President John F. Kennedy used his inaugural address—the speech he made when he took office on January 20, 1961—to challenge Americans to help make the world a better place. Kennedy's speech also sent a message to other world leaders that the United States was committed to fighting against the spread of Communism.

Let the word go forth from this time and place, to friend and foe alike, that the torch has been passed to a new generation of Americans—born in this century, tempered [hardened] by war, disciplined by a hard and bitter peace, proud of our ancient heritage—and unwilling to witness or permit the slow undoing of those human rights to which this nation has always been committed, and to which we are committed today at home and around the world.

Let every nation know, whether it wishes us well or ill, that we shall pay any price, bear any burden, meet any hardship, support any friend, oppose any foe to assure the survival and the success of liberty.

This much we pledge—and more. . . .

In the long history of the world, only a few generations have been granted the role of defending freedom in its hour of maximum danger. I do not shrink from this responsibility—I welcome it. I do not believe that any of us would exchange places with any other people or any other generation. The energy, the faith, the devotion which we bring to this endeavor will light our country and all who serve it—and the glow from that fire can truly light the world.

And so, my fellow Americans: ask not what your country can do for you— ask what you can do for your country.

Along with all that was new and different about the Kennedy administration, there was also much carried over from the past. Since the end of World War II in 1945, U.S. leaders had been concerned about the spread of Communism. As the Soviet Union set up Communist governments throughout Eastern Europe and backed Communist revolutions in China and other countries, a "cold war" had begun—a time of suspicion and hostility between the world's two great superpowers. During the 1950s Americans were afraid that the Soviets were taking over the world. It seemed that the United States was losing the race to launch satellites into space, put a man on the moon, build more and better weapons of mass destruction. Dreading a nuclear war, American families built bomb shelters in their backyards and children practiced air-raid drills at school. To twelve-year-old David Obst of California, the idea of crawling under a desk to "wait for the nuclear firestorm to safely pass over" was stupid . . . and scary. But, like the rest of his classmates, David was

> *passionately anticommunist. In the 50s, good, red-blooded American boys and girls hated the commies. As we sat eating our TV dinners in the den, watching such shows as* I Led Three Lives *[a TV spy series], we were alerted to the Red menace lurking on the horizon.*

One of the areas in the world that American military leaders thought was most threatened by the Communist menace was Southeast Asia. In 1954 President Eisenhower warned that the small countries in that part of the world were like "a row of dominoes. . . . You knock over the first one and what will happen to the last one is the certainty that it will go over very quickly." President Kennedy agreed with this "domino theory." The United States had to take a stand against Communist aggression in Asia, he told one reporter, "and Vietnam looks like the place."

DURING THE COLD WAR, AMERICANS WORRIED ABOUT THE POSSIBILITY OF COMMUNIST ATTACK. CHILDREN WERE TAUGHT TO "PROTECT" THEMSELVES FROM A NUCLEAR BLAST BY HIDING UNDER THEIR SCHOOL DESKS.

Between 1961 and 1963, President Kennedy increased the number of American military advisers in Vietnam from nine hundred to more than sixteen thousand. Gradually the new "advisers" began to take a more active role in the fighting, moving from training South Vietnam's troops to joining them in combat.

BY THE END OF 1963, MORE THAN SIX HUNDRED U.S. MILITARY ADVISERS HAD BEEN KILLED OR WOUNDED IN VIETNAM. GRIEF-STRICKEN AT THE DEATH OF HER BROTHER, BOBBIE LOU PENDERGRASS OF SANTA ANA, CALIFORNIA, WROTE TO PRESIDENT KENNEDY. HER LETTER ASKED QUESTIONS THAT MANY PEOPLE WOULD POSE IN THE YEARS AHEAD: WHY WAS THE UNITED STATES INVOLVED IN A CONFLICT HALFWAY AROUND THE GLOBE, AND WHY WEREN'T AMERICAN GIs BEING GIVEN A FAIR CHANCE TO FIGHT?

February 18, 1963

Dear President Kennedy,

My brother, Specialist James Delmas McAndrew, was one of the seven crew members killed on January 11 in a Viet Nam helicopter crash.

The Army reports at first said that communist gunfire was suspected. Later it said that the helicopter tradgedy was due to malfunction of aircraft controls. I've wondered if the "malfunction of aircraft controls" wasn't due to "communist gunfire." However, that's neither important now, nor do I even care to know.

My two older brothers entered the Navy and the Marine Corps in 1941 immediately after the war [World War II] started—they served all during the war and in some very important battles—then Jim went into the Marines as soon as he was old enough and was overseas for a long time. During those war years and even all during the Korean conflict we worried about all of them—but that was all very different. They were wars that our country was fighting, and everyone here knew that our sons and brothers were giving their lives for their country.

I can't help but feel that giving one's life for one's country is one thing, but being sent to a country where half our country never even heard of and being shot at without even a chance to shoot back is another thing altogether!

Please, I'm only a housewife who doesn't even claim to know all about the international situation—but we have felt so bitter over this—can the small number of our boys over in Viet Nam possibly be doing enough good to justify the awful number of casualties? It seems to me that if we are going to have our boys over there, that we should send enough to have a chance—or else stay home. Those fellows are just sitting ducks in those darn helicopters. If a war is worth fighting—isn't it worth fighting to win?

Please answer this and help me and my family to reconcile ourselves to our loss and to feel that even though Jim died in Viet Nam—and it isn't our war—it wasn't in vain.

I am a good Democrat—and I'm not criticizing. I think you are doing a wonderful job—and God Bless You—

Very sincerely,
Bobbie Lou Pendergrass

Even with American help, President Ngo Dinh Diem's troops continued to lose ground. The problem was that Diem did not have the support of his own people, for his harsh rule had turned many against him. While Diem's soldiers were mostly peasants who had been drafted willingly into the army, the Vietcong—South Vietnamese who supported the Communists—fought fiercely for a cause they believed in.

In the fall of 1963, convinced that a change of leadership was needed, President Kennedy quietly encouraged a group of South Vietnamese generals who were plotting to overthrow their despised leader. Diem was murdered when the generals seized power. In the streets of Saigon, crowds danced and cheered in wild celebration.

Three weeks later President Kennedy himself was assassinated. Americans were plunged into shock and mourning. And a new president, Lyndon B. Johnson, inherited the deepening nightmare of Vietnam.

Into the Hailstorm

"I was relieved to go to Vietnam," says Danny Cruz of Tulsa, Oklahoma. "I wanted to go. I believed it was my duty to serve my country." The first U.S. servicemen engaged in combat in Vietnam believed in their mission. Most were patriotic volunteers determined to do whatever was necessary to keep Southeast Asia safe from the Communists. Philip Caputo, who landed at Da Nang with the first U.S. combat troops sent to Vietnam, remembers the "missionary idealism he [President Kennedy] had awakened in us."

> America seemed omnipotent [all-powerful] then: the country
> could still claim it had never lost a war, and we believed we
> were ordained [appointed] to play cop to the Communists'
> robber and spread our own political faith around the world. . . .
> We carried, along with our packs and rifles, the implicit

convictions [unquestioning beliefs] that the Viet Cong would
be quickly beaten and that we were doing something altogether
noble and good.

WILLIAM EHRHART OF PENNSYLVANIA ALSO VOLUNTEERED FOR MILITARY SERVICE. AT SEVENTEEN, WILLIAM WAS YOUNGER THAN MOST GIs—THE AVERAGE AGE OF THE AMERICAN SERVICEMAN IN VIETNAM WAS NINETEEN. HERE WILLIAM RECALLS HIS DECISION TO JOIN THE U.S. MARINES.

I had been accepted in . . . four colleges, by my senior year. And then I just decided, no, I'm gonna . . . join the Marines. And I had to spend a lot of time talking to my parents about it because at seventeen, of course, I would not have been allowed to sign an enlistment contract in my own right. They had to sign it, too. And really what I think what tipped the scales in the discussion was at one point, after talking for a long time, I said, "Mom, is this the way you raised me, to let other mothers' sons fight America's wars?" And they were young people during World War II. They believed in their country, and that was it. They hadn't raised me that way. . . .

When the government said that the Communists were taking over Vietnam, and if we didn't stop them there we would have to stop them eventually in San Diego, I took that at face value. And I saw my opportunity to really . . . be a hero.

On the homefront, too, Americans overwhelmingly supported their government's stand in Vietnam and approved of President Johnson's handling of the conflict. In 1964 Johnson had been elected to his first full term as president. He had spent much of the past year reassuring a country shaken by the Kennedy assassination and building confidence in his own leadership. Now he hoped to concentrate on a cause close to his heart: fighting poverty and injustice in the United States. Through sweeping programs to protect civil rights, feed the hungry, and improve education, health care, and housing for the disadvantaged, he would build a society in which all Americans had a fair share in their nation's prosperity. But Johnson's dreams for a "Great Society" were quickly overshadowed by what one observer called "that nagging little war in Vietnam."

The leaders who had taken over in South Vietnam after Diem's overthrow had proven just as incapable of waging war. North Vietnam was pouring a steady stream of troops and supplies south, helping the Vietcong increase their hold on the countryside. President Johnson wanted to turn up the pressure on the north. In August 1964 he found a way to accomplish that goal. After receiving reports that North Vietnamese patrol boats might have fired on a U.S. destroyer in the Gulf of Tonkin, off the northern coast, Johnson asked Congress for authority to "take all necessary measures . . . to prevent further aggression." The Tonkin Gulf Resolution was not a formal declaration of war. But it gave the president such broad powers to wage war that he jokingly compared it to "grandma's nightshirt—it covered everything."

In March 1965 President Johnson ordered massive bombings of the north and sent the first 3,500 American combat troops into South Vietnam. Soon more troops were needed to support those already there, and then more. By year's end there were more than 184,000 American GIs in Vietnam.

"I feel like a hitchhiker caught in a hailstorm on a Texas highway," President Johnson confided to an aide. "I can't run. I can't hide. And I can't make it stop." The ceaseless bombing was having no effect, and the buildup of troops and arms only seemed to make the Vietnamese Communists more determined to resist and win. But after pouring so many men and so much firepower into Vietnam, America could not pull out without suffering a

FROM 1965 THROUGH 1968, A BOMBING CAMPAIGN KNOWN AS OPERATION ROLLING
THUNDER BACKED UP U.S. COMBAT TROOPS IN VIETNAM.

humiliating defeat. The only advice military leaders offered was "more": send more soldiers, more equipment, more bombs. To the GIs who had gone to war convinced they'd win a swift and easy victory, the future looked grim. As former marine Philip Caputo put it, "We kept [our] packs and rifles; the convictions, we lost."

On the homefront, where daily news reports told the growing number of U.S. wounded and killed, Americans were beginning to question their government's policy in Vietnam. Those doubts would soon swell into a chorus of protests that would tear the nation apart.

2

THE WAR AT HOME

The weakest chink in our armor is American public opinion. Our people won't stand firm in the face of heavy losses, and they can bring down the government.

—PRESIDENT LYNDON JOHNSON, 1966

Birth of the Antiwar Movement

During every U.S. war there have been Americans who opposed their country's involvement. But opposition to the Vietnam War was different. Never before had so many Americans protested the actions of their government. And never had those protests come from so many different segments of society: young and old, rich and poor, all classes and religions and ethnic groups.

The antiwar movement built slowly. In the 1950s and early 1960s, few Americans objected when increasing numbers of military advisers were sent to Vietnam. Things began to change in 1965, after President Johnson sent in the first combat troops. The president had campaigned as a "peace candidate," vowing that he would not "send American boys nine or ten thousand miles away from home to do what Asian boys ought to be doing for themselves." The troop buildup seemed to turn those promises into lies. The rising number of U.S. casualties heightened concerns. And the brutal images of war broadcast into living rooms across the nation

CROWD OF WOMEN GATHER OUTSIDE DEFENSE DEPARTMENT HEADQUARTERS AT THE
PENTAGON IN WASHINGTON, D.C., TO PROTEST U.S. INVOLVEMENT IN VIETNAM.

every evening served as a final wake-up call. America's first "TV war" brought viewers face-to-face with exploding shells, burning villages, weeping women and children, young GIs wounded or killed. Congress had never formally declared war, but somehow, Americans realized, their country had gotten itself deep into a major war's entanglements.

In March 1965 students and teachers at the University of Michigan held the first "teach-in"—a mass meeting at which dozens of people spoke out against the war. Soon teach-ins were taking place at colleges and universities all across the country. College students had an especially urgent interest in the war—it was their generation doing the fighting and dying. There was another reason much of the energy and inspiration of the antiwar movement centered on college campuses. The students coming of age in the Vietnam years—the baby boomers—had been raised in prosperous times. They took for granted much of what their parents and grandparents had struggled for: a comfortable home, a good education, financial security. They questioned the older generation's traditional values and found fault with American society. Americans, they thought, were materialistic—obsessed with money and possessions. While the United States was the richest country in the world, they saw vast numbers of its people struggling against poverty and injustice.

This new generation of Americans had been influenced by President Kennedy's call to service and by a sense of idealism that made them believe that they could change the world. "The majority of [my class]," explained one student at Brown University in Providence, Rhode Island, "is not content with what it regards as a world badly in need of overhaul."

Many young people turned their discontent into action. Some worked for the civil rights movement that had taken shape in the early 1960s. Hundreds of college students spent their summers down south, where they assisted in voter registration drives and marched against segregation. Barry Clemson, a white student at Pennsylvania State University in 1964–1965, describes the months he spent in Biloxi, Mississippi, registering African-American voters, as a "lesson in courage." Marching with a group of black civil rights protesters, Barry suddenly found himself surrounded by "young white men, lots and lots of them."

> *They were not pleased with us being there. At that point I was the only white face in the crowd so I was sure that I was dead. . . . [A] little old lady . . . took my arm, looked back at the rest of us, and said, "Walk slow and sing loud," and she headed right for the middle of this mob. . . . Everybody else moved back, it was like the Red Sea parting . . . and we went through.*

Other students joined protest movements aimed at a variety of social concerns: banning nuclear weapons, protecting the environment, winning equal rights for women. But by 1965 the war in Vietnam had overshadowed all other causes. To Stan Koper, a student at the University of Michigan, "The society in which we were living seemed upside down—crazy. The war seemed to be craziest of all."

Hawks versus Doves

In April 1965 the first antiwar rally in Washington, D.C., drew 15,000 people. Two years later more than 200,000 protesters marched in New York City and San Francisco. Marches and rallies were just two of the many forms antiwar protests took. There were also picket lines, petitions, and newspaper ads; teach-ins, sit-ins, and "die-ins"—gruesome events at which demonstrators sprawled in the streets like Vietnamese villagers killed by a U.S. air strike.

Letters to Vietnam

Mom, I appreciate all your letters. . . . I'm eager to read anything about what you are doing or the family is doing. . . . For a while, as I read your letters, I am a normal person. I'm not killing people, or worried about being killed.

—Captain Rodney Chastant, South Vietnam, October 19, 1967

To many Americans, the Vietnam War years were a time of bitter divisions that threatened to overwhelm the nation. But to young GIs plunged into a controversial, confusing, deadly conflict far from home, letters to and from loved ones often seemed the only lifeline to a "normal" world.

"The soldiers got a great deal of support from the states," recalls Captain Ted Danielson, looking back on the early years of U.S. involvement. "Classes by the hundreds would write letters addressed to a soldier in Vietnam, and these were packed up and sent to our unit." Larry Skoglund of Minnesota received stacks of mail through a newspaper "Hi GI" program and corresponded with some of the letter writers throughout his service. Of course, GIs also received letters from wives and sweethearts, parents, brothers and sisters, and friends. "A lot of people wrote me letters (and they were the most valuable thing I had over there)," remembers Vietnam veteran Dennis Hodo, "including a sweet little 'girl next door' who I ended up marrying about a year after I got home."

Sometimes the mail carried reactions to major events on the homefront—civil rights clashes, antiwar demonstrations, a presidential pronouncement. More often, though, letters simply carried news of a high school football game, a kid sister's graduation, a friend's wedding—the small, treasured details of everyday life. "You can't understand the importance these 'trivial' [ordinary] events take on out here," U.S. Marine Captain Rodney Chastant wrote to his mother. "Those are the truly important things."

Most mail sent from the homefront to Vietnam has been lost. GIs usually destroyed their letters after reading them, to prevent the enemy from getting hold of personal information that might be used against them if they were captured. The letters that remain—and the personal writings and remembrances of those who lived through the Vietnam years—offer us a valuable firsthand view of those turbulent times.

A SOLDIER WRITES TO HIS WIFE FROM A CAMP OUTSIDE HUE, NEAR THE BORDER OF
NORTH AND SOUTH VIETNAM.

ONE OF THE EARLIEST FORMS OF ANTI-VIETNAM WAR PROTEST WAS DRAFT RESISTANCE. SOME "DRAFT DODGERS" DEFIED THE LAW BY REFUSING TO REGISTER FOR THE MILITARY DRAFT OR BY REGISTERING AND THEN PUBLICLY BURNING THEIR DRAFT ID CARDS. ABOUT 150,000 FLED TO CANADA AND OTHER COUNTRIES THAT WOULD SHELTER THEM. MANY MORE RESISTERS TOOK A SAFER ROUTE, FINDING LOOPHOLES IN THE LAW TO HELP THEM ESCAPE THE DRAFT.

FUTURE PRESIDENT BILL CLINTON BECAME ELIGIBLE FOR THE DRAFT IN 1968, WHILE HE WAS A COLLEGE STUDENT. HE OPPOSED THE WAR BUT FEARED THAT RESISTING THE DRAFT WOULD DESTROY HIS HOPES FOR A FUTURE IN POLITICS. HIS SOLUTION WAS TO SIGN AN AGREEMENT WITH THE ROTC (RESERVE OFFICERS' TRAINING CORPS)—A PROGRAM THAT TRAINS COLLEGE STUDENTS TO BECOME ARMY OFFICERS—WHICH WOULD LET HIM PUT OFF MILITARY SERVICE FOR A YEAR. BY THE TIME THE YEAR ENDED, CHANGES IN THE DRAFT LAW ENSURED THAT HE WOULD NOT BE CALLED TO SERVE. IN THIS LETTER TO THE DIRECTOR OF HIS LOCAL ROTC PROGRAM, CLINTON EXPLAINED HIS CONFLICT AND HIS ACTIONS.

DURING THE VIETNAM WAR, MORE THAN 200,000 YOUNG MEN WERE ACCUSED OF DRAFT OFFENSES THAT INCLUDED BURNING THEIR DRAFT CARDS TO PROTEST THE GOVERNMENT'S WAR POLICY.

December 3, 1969

Dear Colonel Holmes:

. . . First, I want to thank you, not just for saving me from the draft, but for being so kind and decent to me last summer, when I was as low as I have ever been. One thing which made the bond we struck in good faith somewhat palatable [agreeable] to me was my high regard for you personally. . . . The admiration might not have been mutual [shared] had you known a little more about me, about my political beliefs and activities. . . .

Let me try to explain. As you know, I worked for two years in a very minor position on the Senate Foreign Relations Committee. I did it for the experience and the salary but also for the opportunity, however small, of working everyday against a war I opposed and despised with a depth of feeling I had reserved solely for racism in America before Vietnam. . . .

I decided to accept the draft in spite of my beliefs for one reason: to maintain my political viability [ability to succeed] within the system. For years I have worked to prepare myself for a political life. . . . ROTC was the one way left in which I could possibly, but not positively, avoid both Vietnam and resistance. . . .

After I signed the ROTC letter of intent I began to wonder whether the compromise I had made with myself was not more objectionable than the draft would have been, because I had no interest in the ROTC program in itself and all I seemed to have done was to protect myself from physical harm. Also, I began to think I had deceived you. . . . Finally on Sept. 12 I stayed up all night writing a letter to the chairman of my draft board, . . . stating that I couldn't do the ROTC after all and would he please draft me as soon as possible. . . .

I never mailed the letter . . . because I didn't see, in the end, how my going in the army and maybe going to Vietnam would achieve anything except a feeling that I had punished myself and gotten what I had deserved. . . .

And that is where I am now, writing to you because you have been good to me and have a right to know what I think and feel. I am writing too in the hope that my telling you this one story will help you to understand more clearly how so many fine people have come to find themselves still loving their country but loathing the military, to which you and other good men have devoted years, lifetimes, of the best service you could give. To many of us, it is no longer clear what is service and what is disservice, or if it is clear, the conclusion is likely to illegal. . . .

Sincerely,
Bill Clinton

As the antiwar movement grew in size and intensity, it also broadened to include people from all walks of life. Parents marched alongside their children. Farmers and homemakers linked arms with doctors, lawyers, and scientists. Famous baby expert Dr. Benjamin Spock spoke at antiwar rallies. So did Dr. Martin Luther King, Jr., leader of the civil rights movement. Dr. King argued that the war was taking attention and funds away from President Johnson's programs to fight poverty and injustice. "The promises of the Great Society," he thundered, "have been shot down on the battlefield of Vietnam." Thousands of black Americans agreed with Dr. King's criticisms and lent their voices to the antiwar cause.

There was also a large group of Americans who were angered and disturbed by the peace movement. Many members of the older generation who had fought for their country in World War II saw the protesters as unpatriotic and "un-American." These "hawks," as those who supported the war were called, accused the "doves"—those who opposed it—of prolonging the war by giving encouragement to the enemy. Hawks were disgusted with protesting college students, who seemed to be wasting the opportunities handed to them. To one World War II veteran, the students were

bearded leftist brats who demonstrate and riot against America while living off the old man's hard-earned money. . . . Obviously their goal is to destroy the United States of America. This is why patriotic Americans have got to act now to put a stop to all this trouble. You see, we are not only fighting the Communists in Vietnam. We are fighting them within the United States itself.

AT A 1965 ANTIWAR RALLY IN NEW YORK, A HAWK DEMONSTRATES AGAINST THE DEMONSTRATORS.

The sign held by the protester reads:

DEFENDERS OF FREEDOM

REAL MEN

SUPPORT THEIR SACRIFICE

LIFE

A̲S THE WAR IN VIETNAM DRAGGED ON, HAWKS AND DOVES CLASHED—SOMETIMES WITH FISTS BUT MORE OFTEN WITH ANGRY WORDS. MANY PEOPLE WROTE TO THE EDITORS OF THEIR LOCAL NEWSPAPERS, EXPLAINING THEIR SIDE OF THE ISSUE. IN THIS LETTER TO THE LIVINGSTON, NEW JERSEY, *WEST ESSEX TRIBUNE*, JEFF SCHOMP ANSWERED CHARGES MADE BY AN EARLIER LETTER WRITER THAT STUDENTS OPPOSED TO THE WAR WERE TRAITORS TO THEIR COUNTRY. JEFF HAD RECENTLY GRADUATED FROM BROWN UNIVERSITY AND BEEN DRAFTED INTO THE ARMY; HE WOULD SERVE A YEAR WITH THE ELEVENTH ARMORED CAVALRY REGIMENT IN VIETNAM.

West Essex Tribune, Livingston

To the Editor

Vietnam War

Dear sir:

At the risk of starting another sterile argument, and despite the knowledge that every conceivable view of the Vietnam War has already been expressed a depressing number of times with few visible results, I feel compelled to respond to the letter from Sgt. Cartinhour that appeared in your May 22 issue. I wish to make it clear that not everyone in the military views the war as simply part of "the international communist conspiracy," such a view has been repudiated by former Marine Commandant Shoup, Gen. Gavin, and many others. It has been my personal experience that Army service has intensified the antiwar feelings of numerous soldiers.

Does the sergeant think we should "save" South Vietnam, at the cost of thousands of American lives, billions of American dollars, and the resultant social crises in American schools and cities, even if the Vietnamese themselves aren't particularly interested in being saved? It has taken 500,000 American troops fighting for several years merely to gain a costly stalemate; without the intervention the South Vietnamese government surely would have collapsed long ago despite population and resources comparable to those of the North. The point is, are we to commit ourselves to supporting governments with unlimited American blood and money, even if these governments have little or no popular support and little ability or ambition to defend themselves, merely because their leaders proclaim their anti-communism? Communism is certainly still a threat to America; delusions of our omnipotence and an overextension of our power may even be more of a threat.

Not all war opponents are "phoney" or "traitors." Only because I love my country, despite its faults, have I accepted induction and entered into a program which will bring me to Vietnam as a translator.

I would like to think, however, that I am serving a country which tolerates or even encourages freedom of expression and dissent, not one which insists on "kicking out of college" students who question its shortcomings, and which labels its critics "traitors." Or has American democracy with its tradition of freedom of expression become the latest casualty of this tragic war?

Sincerely,
PFC Jeff Schomp
Ft. Bliss, Texas

Dear Sir,

At the risk of starting another sterile [unproductive] argument, . . . I feel compelled to respond to the letter from Sgt. Cartinhour that appeared in your May 22 issue. I wish to make it clear that not everyone in the military views the war as simply part of the "international communist conspiracy." . . . It has been my personal experience that Army service has intensified the antiwar feelings of numerous soldiers.

Does the sergeant think we should "save" South Vietnam, at the cost of thousands of American lives, billions of American dollars, and the resultant social crises in American schools and cities, even if the Vietnamese themselves aren't particularly interested in being saved? It has taken 500,000 American troops fighting for several years merely to gain a costly stalemate [deadlock]; without the intervention the South Vietnamese government surely would have collapsed long ago despite population and resources comparable to those of the North.

The point is, are we to commit ourselves to supporting governments with unlimited American blood and money, even if these governments have little or no popular support and little ability or ambition to defend themselves, merely because their leaders proclaim their anti-communism? Communism is certainly still a threat to America; delusions of our omnipotence [all-powerfulness] and an overextension of our power may even be more of a threat.

Not all war opponents are "phoney" or "traitors." Only because I love my country, despite its faults, have I accepted inductment [enrollment in the army] and entered into a program which will bring me to Vietnam as a translator.

I would like to think, however, that I am serving a country which tolerates or even encourages freedom of expression and dissent, not one which insists on "kicking out of college" students who question its shortcomings, and which labels its critics "traitors." Or has American democracy with its tradition of freedom of expression become the latest casualty of this tragic war?

Sincerely,
PFC [Private First Class] Jeff Schomp
Ft. Bliss, Texas

As hawks and doves clashed more and more, the conflict on the homefront intensified. At antiwar rallies peace marchers were pelted with rotten fruits and eggs. Angry shouting sometimes led to brawling with fists and clubs. One Defense Department official, looking back to Civil War times, cautioned that the divisions "taking place in the United States [hold the] seeds of the worst split in our people in more than a century."

M ANY GIs SERVING IN VIETNAM FELT BETRAYED BY THE ANTIWAR PROTESTS. SOME WROTE LETTERS TO THEIR LOCAL NEWSPAPERS, EXPLAINING WHY THEY HAD CHOSEN TO SERVE. AFTER DENNIS GIUNTA WROTE TO A LONG ISLAND, NEW YORK, NEWSPAPER WHILE SERVING WITH THE NINTH INFANTRY DIVISION IN VIETNAM, HE RECEIVED AS MANY AS FIFTY LETTERS A DAY FROM THE HOMEFRONT. MOST OF THESE WRITERS VOICED THEIR SUPPORT FOR U.S. SERVICEMEN—PROOF THAT, DESPITE THE GROWING ANTIWAR MOVEMENT, MILLIONS OF AMERICANS YOUNG AND OLD STILL SUPPORTED THE WAR AND ITS WARRIORS.

Dear Dennis:

. . . You don't know me or I you but since your address was in the LI Press I figured I'd drop you a line of Thanks for what? Well for one thing doing your part in Vietnam!

It may seem funny to you that a girl should Thank you for doing your part but I am sure serious & If I saw you I'd probably be tempted to shake your hand [. Y]ou guys over in Vietnam deserve the best I think but at the present time The only thing I can offer you are my Letters. I know how hard it is for you men to be away from your family & the Things you love the best. But just Think Dennis Helping to keep the people of your country free *from Communism is something I Look up to you for. I respect you because you didn't run Like any of these draft dodgers over here. I know the people of Long Island are very proud of you.*

They may not know you or your family but you've got friends all over & I am one of them! so keep your chin up *but at The same time keep your* head down! *. . .*

Sincerely
Your friend
Rita

"Burn, Baby, Burn!"

"I shall not seek, and I will not accept, the nomination of my party for another term as your President." In March 1968 President Johnson startled the nation by calling off his campaign for reelection. The president was exhausted by the debate over Vietnam and stung by the sharp criticisms being lobbed at his administration, some by former supporters and members of his own political party. Polls taken at the end of 1967 showed that, for the first time, more Americans opposed their government's policy in Vietnam than supported it.

Some of the new "doves" had simply lost faith in America's ability to win in Vietnam. Two months earlier millions had sat glued to their TV sets, watching scenes of the Tet offensive, the largest and bloodiest battle of the war. Though Tet ended in a U.S.

EXHAUSTED BY THE STRAIN OF FIGHTING AN UNPOPULAR WAR, PRESIDENT LYNDON JOHNSON DECIDED NOT TO SEEK REELECTION IN 1968.

victory, nearly four thousand GIs were killed. Americans who had trusted government assurances that the war was nearly over now wondered how many more years and more lives it would claim. They began to believe that the country had too many problems at home to continue waging this costly, seemingly endless fight.

The United States seemed to be teetering on the brink of self-destruction. After years of protest with no results, the antiwar forces were frustrated and angry. Increasingly, peace marches and rallies ended in illegal sit-ins, the storming of government buildings, and ugly confrontations with war supporters and with the police.

Some protesters began calling for a revolution—the violent overthrow of the U.S. government, which they had come to see as too flawed to fix. Though extremists like these were always a small

AS THE WAR CONTINUED, PROTESTS—AND THE POLICE RESPONSE TO THEM—GREW INCREASINGLY ANGRY AND VIOLENT.

minority, their loud accusations and demands added fuel to the fires already burning on college campuses. In 1968 nearly five hundred universities were rocked by student strikes and protests; many were forced to temporarily shut down. After a student take-over at Columbia University in New York City ended in violence and arrests, protest organizer Mark Rudd warned the university's president that the students were "out for social and political revolution, nothing less."

> *You are quite right in feeling that the situation is "potentially dangerous." For if we win, we will take control of your world . . . and attempt to mold a world in which we and other people can live as human beings. . . . We will have to destroy at times, even violently, in order to end your power and your system.*

REBEL STUDENTS FORM A "HUMAN BARRICADE" AROUND COLUMBIA UNIVERSITY DURING THE 1968 TAKEOVER. THE STUDENTS WERE PROTESTING THE UNIVERSITY'S RACIAL POLICIES AND ITS ROLE IN MILITARY RESEARCH.

In April 1968 Martin Luther King was assassinated. Black students boycotted their classes and riots exploded in more than a hundred cities, with enraged African Americans smashing windows, looting stores, and setting fires, all to the cry of "Burn, baby, burn!" Two months later the nation again reeled in shock when Robert Kennedy, brother of the former president and a top contender for the Democratic presidential nomination, was also assassinated.

Kennedy's death cleared the way for another leading Democratic candidate, Vice President Hubert Humphrey. The vice president supported President Johnson's Vietnam policy. Members of the antiwar movement vowed to protest his nomination by disrupting the Democratic National Convention. Five thousand demonstrators showed up outside the convention hall in Chicago, only to find themselves confronted by a force of twelve thousand police. The demonstrators threw rocks, bottles, and urine-filled

VICE PRESIDENT HUBERT HUMPHREY, A SUPPORTER OF PRESIDENT JOHNSON'S VIETNAM POLICY, WON THE DEMOCRATIC PARTY'S NOMINATION FOR PRESIDENT IN 1968.

A VIOLENT FREE-FOR-ALL BETWEEN DEMONSTRATORS AND POLICE AT THE DEMOCRATIC CONVENTION OF 1968 LED MANY AMERICANS TO SHIFT THEIR VOTES TO THE REPUBLICAN PRESIDENTIAL CANDIDATE, RICHARD NIXON.

balloons. Finally, the police charged into the crowd and began clubbing anyone they could get their hands on—demonstrators, reporters, convention delegates, innocent passersby. To student David Obst, caught in the middle of the free-for-all, the police were "a pack of wolves. Clubs beat onto skulls with sickening thuds. I had never been so scared in my life." To Americans watching on TV, it looked like the end of law and order in America. Disgusted, many people switched their support to the Republican Party's nominee, Richard Nixon.

Nixon won the 1968 presidential election. He had campaigned promising to bring a speedy end to war, but years of fighting and dying still lay ahead. And on the American homefront, divisions over Vietnam, racial discrimination, and a host of other issues would only deepen.

THE CIVIL RIGHTS MOVEMENT

I remember once when I was in sixth grade and . . . some white children were fighting a black girl. And I think the black girl really got the best of them because she was kind of a tough girl, you know. You just didn't run over Geneva. . . . The next day some white men came to our school and told the professor that they wanted to take Geneva I don't know where. . . . And the principal let them go, let the child go, and they beat the child up. . . . Well, at that time, black people just didn't go against white people.

—CIVIL RIGHTS WORKER CONSTANCE BAKER

A Dream of Justice

On a fall day in 1962, a black air force veteran stepped onto the University of Mississippi campus. James Meredith intended to become the first African American to enroll at the all-white university. A crowd of white Southerners planned to stop him. Suddenly violence erupted. The mob hurled bricks, rocks, and firebombs at the federal marshals sent by President Kennedy to protect Meredith. By the time the riot ended, two people had been killed and more than eighty wounded—all because a black man tried to exercise his right to seek a good education.

THE CIVIL RIGHTS MOVEMENT FOUGHT TO END SEGREGATION—THE PRACTICE THAT SET UP SEPARATE AND OFTEN INFERIOR SCHOOLS, HOUSING, AND PUBLIC FACILITIES FOR BLACK AMERICANS.

By the 1960s the United States had long been a land of racial inequality and injustice. African Americans were routinely denied the right to vote, to receive equal treatment under the law, to compete on equal terms with whites for good jobs, housing, and education. Segregation kept the races separate—and kept blacks at the bottom of the social ladder. Former civil rights worker Constance Baker of Hattiesburg, Mississippi, recalls the frustration of not being allowed inside the local "whites-only" library. "For instance, if I wanted to check out a book on black history, I couldn't do it because I was black. . . . I had to get some white person that I knew to . . . check out that book in her name and just let me read it." Vietnam veteran Norman McDaniel, who grew up in Fayetteville, North Carolina, describes his hometown as "no different from most of the other cities in the South and some in the North."

You couldn't go in restaurants. You rode in the back of the bus.
And there were separate sections and toilets for the black people
in bus stations and train stations. I went to a segregated ele-
mentary and high school. . . . There was a bus stop to pick up
white students about a block and a half from where I lived, but
I would have to walk 5 miles to get the bus for black students.

African Americans had begun to challenge segregation in the early 1950s. Their protests grew into the civil rights movement. With his gift for expressive, inspiring speech, Martin Luther King emerged as a leader of that movement. The young black minister urged his followers to use nonviolent action to combat racial hatred and "the stinging darts of segregation." Under his guidance civil rights protesters staged peaceful sit-ins at lunch counters, libraries, and other public places that refused to serve blacks. They

WAITRESSES IGNORE TWO AFRICAN-AMERICAN COLLEGE STUDENTS AT A SIT-IN AT A NORTH CAROLINA "WHITES ONLY" LUNCH COUNTER IN 1960.

boycotted city buses until the laws requiring African Americans to ride in the back were changed. They organized "freedom rides," traveling from state to state throughout the south to protest segregated buses and bus terminals.

Though civil rights demonstrations were peaceful, they often met with violence. Freedom riders were dragged from their buses and beaten. Civil rights workers were clubbed, shot at, and arrested on phony charges. The homes, schools, and churches of southern blacks were bombed and burned. In April 1963, when Martin Luther King led a peaceful protest march through Birmingham, Alabama, the demonstrators were attacked by local police. As horrified Americans watched on TV, unarmed men, women, and children were beaten with clubs, shocked with electric cattle prods, and mauled by snarling police dogs. Nearly 2,500 demonstrators were arrested, including Dr. King.

FREEDOM RIDERS IN ALABAMA RECOVER FROM AN ATTACK BY A WHITE MOB, WHICH STONED THEIR BUS, SLASHED THE TIRES, AND SET IT ON FIRE.

WHILE IN JAIL FOLLOWING HIS ARREST, DR. KING READ A STATEMENT BY A GROUP OF LOCAL WHITE MINISTERS THAT HAD BEEN PUBLISHED IN A BIRMINGHAM NEWSPAPER. THE MINISTERS CALLED FOR AN END TO THE DEMONSTRATIONS, ASKING AFRICAN AMERICANS TO SHOW MORE PATIENCE AND "COMMON SENSE" IN PRESSING THEIR DEMANDS. SCRIBBLING A REPLY IN THE MARGINS OF THE NEWSPAPER AND ON OTHER SCRAPS OF PAPER, THE CIVIL RIGHTS LEADER EXPLAINED HIS PEOPLE'S "LEGITIMATE AND UNAVOIDABLE IMPATIENCE" FOR EQUALITY AND JUSTICE.

April 16, 1963

My Dear Fellow Clergymen:

While confined here in the Birmingham city jail, I came across your recent statement calling my present activities "unwise and untimely.". . . I want to try to answer your statement. . . .

You deplore [disapprove of] the demonstrations taking place in Birmingham. But your statement, I am sorry to say, fails to express a similar concern for the conditions that brought about the demonstrations. . . .

We know through painful experience that freedom is never voluntarily given by the oppressor; it must be demanded by the oppressed. Frankly, I have yet to engage in a direct-action campaign that was "well timed" in the view of those who have not suffered unduly from the disease of segregation. For years now I have heard the word "Wait!" It rings in the ear of every Negro with piercing familiarity. This "Wait" has almost always meant "Never." . . .

Perhaps it is easy for those who have never felt the stinging darts of segregation to say, "Wait." But when you have seen vicious mobs lynch your mothers and fathers at will and drown your sisters and brothers at whim; when you have seen hate-filled policemen curse, kick and even kill your black brothers and sisters; when you see the vast majority of your twenty million Negro brothers smothering in an airtight cage of poverty in the midst of an affluent [wealthy] society; when you suddenly find your tongue twisted and your speech stammering as you seek to explain to your six-year-old daughter why she can't go to the public amusement park that has just been advertised on television, and see tears welling up in her eyes when she is told that Funtown is closed to colored children, . . . when you are humiliated day in and day out by nagging signs reading "white" and "colored"; . . . when you are forever fighting a degenerating [sinking] sense of "nobodiness"—then you will understand why we find it difficult to wait. . . .

Yours for the cause of Peace and Brotherhood,

Martin Luther King, Jr.

Following the Birmingham demonstrations, President Kennedy called for the most sweeping civil rights bill in American history. Martin Luther King organized a march on Washington to rally support for the bill. Speaking before a crowd of nearly a quarter of a million people, Dr. King delivered what would become his most famous speech:

> I have a dream that one day this nation will rise up and live out the true meaning of its creed: "We hold these truths to be self-evident, that all men are created equal." I have a dream that one day on the red hills of Georgia, the sons of former slaves and the sons of former slave owners will be able to sit down together at the table of brotherhood. . . . I have a dream

CIVIL RIGHTS LEADER MARTIN LUTHER KING, JR., ORGANIZED NONVIOLENT ACTIONS, MARCHES, AND DEMONSTRATIONS TO BREAK THE "CHAINS OF DISCRIMINATION."

that my four little children will one day live in a nation where they will not be judged by the color of their skin but by the content of their character.

In 1964 President Lyndon Johnson pushed the Civil Rights Act through Congress. The new law outlawed segregation in schools and public facilities and created job opportunities for blacks. It was a key element of Johnson's Great Society programs. But it created barely a ripple in the great pool of black poverty and oppression. Soon even that small hope for progress would be swallowed up in the rising costs of America's war in Vietnam.

Black Power!

From 1965 to 1968 the United States suffered the worst racial violence in its history. African Americans had grown bitter as the war in Vietnam devoured the funds promised for President Johnson's programs to fight poverty and racial injustice. Civil rights leaders had spoken out against the war, and polls showed that blacks were twice as likely as whites to oppose it. In some ways the antiwar movement and the civil rights movement had merged, joining forces to work toward a shared goal.

But African Americans had more on their minds than just Vietnam. Since the very beginnings of the civil rights movement, they had watched white racists answer their peaceful demands for change with brutal violence. Innocent men, women, and children had been murdered. There seemed to be no end to the hatred and injustice. Some blacks began to question the policy of nonviolent resistance that had been the guiding light of their cause. Members of the Black Panther Party, a militant black movement organized in the mid-1960s, demanded "an immediate end to police brutality and murder of black people." "We must move from resistance to aggression," proclaimed Black Panther officer H. Rap Brown, "from revolt to revolution!"

Another radical black leader to come on the scene was Malcolm X, a minister of the militant Black Muslim movement and, later, a founder of the Organization of Afro-American Unity. The Black Muslims believed that the races could never get along and demanded the establishment of a separate black nation within the United States. After a racist mob attacked peaceful demonstrators led by Martin Luther King in Florida, Malcolm X sent this telegram, urging Dr. King to take a more forceful stand.

1964 JUN 30

DR. MARTIN LUTHER KING
ST AUGUSTINE FLA

WE HAVE BEEN WITNESSING WITH
GREAT CONCERN THE VICIOUS
ATTACKS OF THE WHITE RACES
AGAINST OUR POOR DEFENSELESS
PEOPLE THERE IN ST AUGUSTINE.
IF THE FEDERAL GOVERNMENT WILL
NOT SEND TROOPS TO YOUR AID,
JUST SAY THE WORD AND WE WILL
IMMEDIATELY DISPATCH SOME OF
OUR BROTHERS THERE TO ORGANIZE
SELF DEFENSE UNITS AMONG OUR
PEOPLE AND THE KLU [KU] KLUX
KLAN WILL THEN RECEIVE A TASTE
OF ITS OWN MEDICINE. THE DAY OF
TURNING THE OTHER CHEEK TO
THOSE BRUTE BEASTS IS OVER.

MALCOLM X

THE ORGANIZATION OF
AFRO-AMERICAN UNITY
MALCOLM–X CHAIRMAN

A Two-Front War

The black serviceman in Vietnam fought two wars: one against the Vietnamese Communists, the other against a more familiar enemy, racism. "You could go aboard a carrier with 5,000 people," says retired U.S. Navy Lieutenant Commander William S. Norman, "and you would find the overwhelming majority of the blacks in the lowest level in jobs, in the dirtiest jobs, down in the laundry room, down in the bowels of the ship." One of the few African Americans who rose to high military rank during the war, Norman remembers walking "into the areas where I work[ed] with all the sophisticated computers, and it would look as if there were no blacks on the entire ship."

In 1965 blacks made up about 10 percent of U.S. troops in Vietnam—roughly the same proportion as their population back home—but accounted for more than 20 percent of combat deaths. That was because black soldiers were much more likely than whites to be sent on dangerous assignments with frontline combat troops. In time the military corrected those imbalances. Black and white servicemen were spread more evenly through combat and noncombat roles. But black servicemen like Bob Sanders, a paratrooper with the 173rd Infantry, were left feeling "that they put us on the front lines abroad and in the back lines at home."

As racial tensions heated up on the American homefront, conflicts between black and white servicemen also increased. The men generally cooperated in combat zones, where they needed one another's help to survive. But in the base camps—the fortified camps where GIs rested after operations in the field—insults flew between the races, sometimes leading to fights with fists or knives. Paratrooper Bob Sanders "just wanted no part of the war. . . . We felt that blacks should not have had to fight in Vietnam if, when they got home, they couldn't even get a job." Looking back on his years with the navy, William Norman reflects that black servicemen "paid a special price. . . . Those who experienced the racism in a war we lost wear a scar. Vietnam left a scar on them that won't go away."

A U.S. MACHINE GUNNER IN VIETNAM, 1968. MANY AFRICAN-AMERICAN GIs FELT BITTER WHEN DISCRIMINATION FOLLOWED THEM TO WAR, PLACING MORE BLACKS THAN WHITES IN COMBAT.

To African Americans in northern cities, talk of civil rights and peaceful resistance often had little meaning. Forced to live in run-down ghettos, amid poverty, unemployment, and inferior housing and schools, many of these people welcomed the radicals' cries of "Black Power!" and "Revolution!" In August 1965 their frustration and rage boiled over. In the Watts ghetto of Los Angeles, California, a scuffle between police and two young black men mushroomed into a riot that raged for six days. Some ten thousand rioters looted white-owned businesses, set whole city blocks ablaze, and drove off police and firefighters with rocks, bottles, and bullets.

ONE YOUNG MAN LIVING IN THE WATTS GHETTO, A TEENAGER WE KNOW ONLY AS "MEL," LATER TALKED ABOUT THE CHAOS AND DESTRUCTION.

At first I was really frightened, because I had heard about riots in other countries, but never a riot in America. Never had I realized what a riot really was. So I went in the store, and I was panicky. Everybody was knocking down, peoples grabbing stuff, . . . stuff was all over the floor; people were just taking what they want.

Little kids was all out on the streets. Peoples were shooting guns, and the sky was just black, like the world was going to come to an end. People was running out, and there was this one lady, she was hollering, "Stop, you peoples don't know what you're doin.'" . . .

People was turning over people's cars. . . . They ran over to the gas station. . . . They started takin' gas out of the pump, putting 'em in Coca-Cola bottles, and beer bottles, and anything they could, big jugs, and scratchin' a match, and puttin' it to it, and throwin' it to a car, and blowin' it up. . . .

I saw cars with kids, this is what made me want to stop, because I saw little kids, seven or eight years old, Caucasian [white] kids, in the cars flying down the street. Their fathers, their mothers, were driving; they had big holes in their heads, and all the windows were broken out of their cars. . . . I saw one boy run after a car and had a big two by four in his hand, and the man came out, he was shooting a gun. He was just starting to shoot; the boy, he hit him across the head with the two by four and five or six other ones just beat him to death. . . . It was just horrible.

ARMED NATIONAL GUARDSMEN PATROL THE STREETS OF NEWARK, NEW JERSEY, AFTER THREE DAYS OF RIOTS AND LOOTING.

The fiery scenes in Watts would be repeated again and again over the next three summers. Riots ravaged Detroit, Michigan; Newark, New Jersey; Washington, D.C.; and hundreds of other northern cities. Worst of all was the violence that followed the assassination of Martin Luther King in Memphis, Tennessee, in April 1968. In a strange and disturbing twist, the death of the foremost champion of nonviolence ignited riots in 63 cities, leaving at least 46 people dead, more than 2,600 injured, and some $67 million in property damage.

By the end of the 1960s, the rioting had run its course. Most of the leaders of the black militant groups had been killed or arrested. And many African Americans had come to realize that, when their neighborhoods were destroyed in racial violence, they themselves were the greatest victims. "Why should [rioters] burn up Washington, D.C., for something that happened in Memphis?" asked Vietnam veteran Archie "Joe" Biggers. "They didn't hurt the white man. . . . They hurt the black man."

Gradually voters began to elect African Americans to political offices. Blacks began to serve as mayors and sit on city councils and boards of education. The call for a black revolution gave way to a quiet determination to try to work once again within the system. Even former radicals such as Reginald Edwards, once a leader of the Washington, D.C., chapter of the Black Panthers, got tired of people who only wanted to "kick whitey's ass. We didn't think about buying property or gaining economic independence. . . . It's pretty obvious that you don't have to have guns to get power. People get things out of this country and they don't stick up America to do it."

Many problems still remained. And many instances of discrimination, injustice, and poverty are with us even today. But as Archie "Joe" Biggers put it, "We are part of America. Even though there have been some injustices made, there is no reason for us not to be part of the American system."

"WOMEN ARISE"

Women have accepted oppression for so long that it's extremely important to make it clear they are not going to accept it any longer. When you spit on a person, you're not trying to drown him; you're just trying to let him know that you don't like him. And women have to let this system know they don't like it!

—FLORYNCE KENNEDY, SEPTEMBER 1970

The "Weaker Sex"

The struggle for women's rights in the United States is as old as the country itself. In 1776, when the Founding Fathers met to form a new nation, Abigail Adams urged her husband, John, to *"remember the ladies. . . . We . . . will not hold ourselves bound by any laws in which we have no voice or representation."* Despite Abigail's pleas, the U.S. Constitution denied American women their voice. It would take nearly 150 years for feminists—supporters of women's rights—to force Congress to pass the Nineteenth Amendment to the Constitution, granting women the right to vote.

In the 1960s conditions were ripe for a new women's rights movement. Americans were marching for peace, rallying for civil rights, and proclaiming the power of the people to change society. Women were a part of all these struggles. But they were almost always stuck with the lowest-level jobs: stuffing envelopes, answering telephones, serving coffee to the men. "Women made peanut butter," sneered one male antiwar activist. "They waited on tables, cleaned up." To one woman working for an environmentalist group,

A WOMEN'S LIBERATION PARADE IN NEW YORK, 1971. DURING THE VIETNAM WAR YEARS, WOMEN STAGED MARCHES, SIT-INS, AND STRIKES TO DEMAND EQUALITY IN WORK, EDUCATION, AND THE LAW.

"Licking stamps began to taste like licking boots." A black woman disgusted with her lowly role in a civil rights organization found herself asking, "Power to *what* people?"

Women's second-class status in protest movements was a reflection of the inequality of the sexes in American society. Most people believed that women were the "weaker sex"—more dependent and less capable than men. While the man's role was to protect and support his family, women were expected to stay at home and devote their lives to pleasing their husbands and taking care of their children. TV and magazine ads showed these "happy housewives" humming contentedly as they scrubbed the kitchen sink, tackled ring around the collar, and smoothed on a new skin cream promising eternal youth and "a deep sense of fulfillment."

"In the magazine image," said feminist leader Betty Friedan, "women do no work except housework and work to keep their bodies beautiful and to get and keep a man."

IN THE EARLY 1960s JOURNALIST BETTY FRIEDAN CONDUCTED A SURVEY OF AMERICAN WOMEN AND FOUND THAT MOST WERE DEEPLY DISSATISFIED WITH LIVES THAT LIMITED THEM TO THE ROLE OF WIFE-MOTHER-HOMEMAKER. FRIEDAN PUBLISHED HER FINDINGS IN *THE FEMININE MYSTIQUE*. THIS WISCONSIN HOMEMAKER, WHOSE NAME IS UNKNOWN, WAS JUST ONE OF THE THOUSANDS OF WOMEN WHO WROTE TO THANK FRIEDAN FOR PUTTING INTO WORDS FEELINGS THAT THEY HAD BEEN UNABLE OR AFRAID TO EXPRESS.

I am grateful because you have dispelled [driven away] some of the loneliness I have felt in a lifetime struggle for knowledge and achievement. And given me an incentive [motive] to continue, for one begins to think it is time to lie quietly in the grave when clods of dirt keep plopping you in the face. I married at nineteen, a junior in college—completed my B.A. [Bachelor of Arts degree] at twenty-three, a mother of one, obtained another year of college and a teaching certificate at twenty-six, the mother of two. I could not believe that the pleasure I gained teaching a classroom of young people was neurotic [abnormal], nor did it seem apart from my own "femininity," whatever that is. But I met with hostility everywhere. . . . Parents, husband, other women, an occasional professor, sometimes a colleague [coworker]. So I fought in addition to hostility a sense of guilt which caused me to do all my own housework in spite of the demands of my job—and for some time, for the simple pleasure of teaching I renounced [gave up] all social life and recreation in order to spend time with my children. My regret is the fatigue, the sorrow, the emotional drain spent in an effort to be what I am. . . . You see, one can struggle . . . for only so long. I had been ready (from fatigue, perhaps) to pitch it all, convinced that after all THEY must be right—devotion and another go at the kitchen floor are the answer and [I] have been just ready to turn my two independent, vital and charming daughters into the kitchen where all of society seems to want them to be.

BETTY FRIEDAN, A "FOUNDING MOTHER" OF THE MODERN WOMEN'S MOVEMENT. FRIEDAN'S BOOK *THE FEMININE MYSTIQUE* ATTACKED THE IDEA THAT WOMEN CAN ONLY FIND FULFILLMENT THROUGH HOMEMAKING AND RAISING CHILDREN.

Most women who worked outside the home—and that included 38 percent of all American women in 1960—held low-paying jobs: secretary, sales clerk, typist, waitress, maid. Even those few who managed to climb the career ladder to become scientists, lawyers, or college professors were paid far less than men performing the same work. In 1965 a U.S. Department of Labor study showed that the average wage for women was only 60 percent of that earned by men.

In many states labor laws—originally intended to protect the "weaker sex"—reinforced the discrimination. "In 36 states working hours for women are regulated," reported *Life* magazine,

> and in 20 of these, where they are expressly prohibited from working more than eight hours a day or 48 hours a week, they are thus protected from the opportunity of earning any substantial overtime pay or promotion to jobs requiring much overtime. In 26 states women are not permitted to enter certain occupations or industries. . . . In Michigan, one section of the code states: "No female shall be given any task disproportionate [excessive] to her strength, nor shall she be employed in any place detrimental [damaging] to her morals, her health, or her capacity for motherhood."

There were also state regulations prohibiting women from renting a hotel room, entering a bar or restaurant without a male escort, or starting a business without their husband's consent. Laws like these played "a leading role in oppressing women,"

Women at War

While American women fought for equal rights on the homefront, 7,500 of their sisters were waging a very different battle in Vietnam. Some of the women in the U.S. military served as mapmakers, decoders, air traffic controllers, supply clerks, or translators. Most, though, belonged to the U.S. Army Nurse Corps. Army nurses often worked in combat zones, in constant danger of enemy attack. They faced an endless horror show of crippling wounds, pain, and death. Twelve years after the war's end, Anne Simon Auger talked about the emotional costs of serving as a nurse in Vietnam.

The patient that chased me off the ward . . . was a lieutenant named . . . I don't remember his last name—his first name was John. He was twenty-one. He'd gotten married just before he came to Vietnam. And he was shot in his face. He absolutely lost his entire face from ear to ear. He had no nose. He was blind. It didn't matter, I guess, because he was absolutely a vegetable. He was alive and breathing; tubes and machines were keeping him alive. . . . I just . . . I couldn't handle it. To think of how one instant had affected his life. . . . His wife's life was completely changed, his parents, his friends, me—it affected me too. And all because of one split second. I got to realizing how vulnerable [open to attack] everybody was. And how vulnerable I was. I took care of him for a week. They finally shipped him to Japan, and I never heard from him again. I don't know if he's dead or alive. I don't know how his wife or his family are doing. I don't know how he's doing. It seems like every patient on that ward, when they left, took a piece of me with them. They came in, we would treat them for a few hours or a few days, and then we'd send them off and never hear a word. I had this real need to see one GI who'd survived the war after an injury, because I never saw them—never heard from them again. There was one time in Vietnam when I came so close to writing to my mother and asking her to check around and see if she could find one whole eighteen-year-old. I didn't believe we could have any left.

argued feminist lawyer Florynce Kennedy. "Try to rent an apartment without a husband's (or some man's) signature. I can't begin to tell how many times a woman, separated from her husband, had to get him to sign a lease or help her get a charge account."

The New Feminists

"I did not set out consciously to start a revolution," said Betty Friedan, looking back on the furor caused by her book *The Feminine Mystique*, "but it changed my life, as a woman and as a writer, and other women tell me it changed theirs." Many historians consider the publication of Friedan's book the start of the modern women's liberation movement. So many women responded to the book's call for equality and freedom of choice that Friedan and other feminist leaders decided to organize "a new movement toward . . . a fully equal partnership of the sexes."

Founded in 1966, NOW (the National Organization for Women) quickly became one of the largest and most powerful political action groups in the country. NOW's members battled sex discrimination in the workplace, forcing newspapers to stop listing job openings in columns labeled, "Help Wanted—Male" and "Help Wanted—Female." They won court cases overturning state laws that barred women from traditionally male jobs such as bartender, truck driver, firefighter, and airline pilot. They persuaded Congress to pass the Equal Rights Amendment—a proposed Constitutional amendment outlawing discrimination on account of sex.

By the beginning of the 1970s, millions of women belonged to NOW or to one of the many smaller women's groups that had sprung up all over the country. Local groups devoted their energies to solving a community's specific problems and needs: building a women's health clinic or a shelter for battered wives, starting a day care center or a women's self-defense class, pressing a school to spend as much on girls' sports teams as it did on boys'. Women also joined forces to organize marches and demonstrations to demand equality. The largest of these was held on Women's Strike for Equality Day, August 26, 1970, the fiftieth anniversary of the passage of the Nineteenth Amendment. Under the headline WOMEN ARISE, a *Life* magazine article described the demonstrations held that day in nearly every major American city as a "revolution that will affect everybody. . . . There were few who saw or heard them who doubted the iron resolve of the new feminists, or the justice of their cause."

Not everyone supported the women's liberation movement. Surprisingly, some of its most bitter opponents were women themselves. Many of these antifeminists disagreed with the feminists' support of legalized abortion. Others thought that the "women's libbers" were too loud, too pushy, too "unfeminine." "For the life of me, I cannot understand why the [feminists] who are most active and radical must also be so vulgar and unladylike," said Lucy Rankin of Lancaster, Pennsylvania. A California homemaker complained that she was "sick of having my station in life referred to as trapped. . . . I happen to love the rewards of being completely passive [not aggressive]. . . . I don't want to compete with my husband." To Phyllis Schlafly, leader of a movement opposing the Equal Rights Amendment (ERA), feminists were just spoiled women with "distorted minds." Schlafly and her supporters saw the women's movement as "a total assault on the role of the American woman as wife and mother, and on the family as the basic unit of society."

Though Congress had passed the ERA, the amendment was never ratified, or approved, by enough states to become part of the Constitution. When the deadline for ratification passed in 1982, some people said that the women's movement was dead. Betty Friedan and other feminists answered, "Not by a long shot." Feminism had brought great strides toward full equality for women. In the thirty years since the ERA's passage, changes in federal and state laws have given women most of the rights and protections the amendment would have ensured. And there have been other changes, deep in the fabric of American society, in the way women and men see themselves and each other. "There could be no going back," said feminist writer Flora Davis,

for a generation of women used to seeing female police officers, doctors, and lawyers, used to women in the military, in the pulpit, in space, and almost everywhere else. . . . Though they might take women's gains for granted, they [aren't] likely to surrender them without a fight because they [believe] that women [have] a right to them. Whether they [know] it or not, that belief was a gift from the women's movement.

"My Nightmares Never Seem to Go Away"

The Vietnam War years were a time of exciting new challenges and opportunities for women. But for those with husbands, sons, or brothers serving in Vietnam, loneliness and worry overshadowed all other concerns. When a loved one died in action, life changed forever. Nearly thirty years after the death of her son Thomas, an army private who died in Vietnam in 1966, Helen Hightower still grieved, and found some comfort in hearing from the men who served with him.

Nov. 22, 1993

Dear Gary,

I received your letter a couple of days ago. I have also had letters from Luther Kantner, George Robinson, Mack Forgey and the acting Sr. Chaplain, Archie Roberts.

I can't begin to tell you how much these letters mean to me. I still grieve for my son as I'm sure all mothers do. It's so good to hear his buddies tell me about him. He was 23 years old when he lost his life. He would have been 24 in just one more month.

I guess the reason I requested information about my son is I just can't seem to let go. Also, I have wondered if he suffered when he was shot or if it was instant. My nightmares never seem to go away.

My heart goes out to all of you wonderful men who served in Viet Nam. During the war over there, there were many demonstrations. I was furious. To think my son, and others were over there fighting for people like that.

Tommy, (as we called him) was buried in Klamath Falls, Oregon, with full military honors. . . .

We were able to see our son before he was burried, for which I was greatful.

Gary, I thank you again for your kindness and also for the pictures you sent. I always wondered what it was like over there.

I haven't made it to Washington to see the Memorial but hope to see it soon and I thank you also for thinking of Tommy when you are there. I do have some rubbings that other people have given me while there.

Please forgive any mistakes etc. I have arthritis in my hands and can't type any more. With much gratitude and fondness,

Sincerely,
Helen Hightower

THESE LETTERS WRITTEN TO A LOVED ONE IN VIETNAM WERE RETURNED UNDELIVERED WHEN THE GI WAS REPORTED MISSING IN ACTION.

AFTER 5 DAYS RETURN TO
RETURNED TO WRITER
VIA AIR MAIL
REASON CHECKED
VERIFIED MISSING IN ACTION
E. L. ASHLEY, CAPT
Chief, Casualty Branch
Hq 2d Air Division

5

A BITTER PEACE

Tin soldiers and Nixon comin'
We're finally on our own
This summer I hear the drummin'
Four dead in Ohio

—"OHIO,"
CROSBY, STILLS, NASH, AND YOUNG
(SONG WRITTEN AFTER THE
KENT STATE UNIVERSITY SHOOTINGS)

The Counterculture Revolution

In January 1969 Richard Nixon was sworn in as president of a bitterly divided nation. Americans were choosing sides: hawk versus dove, black versus white, feminist versus antifeminist. Widest of all was the gulf between the younger and older generations.

On one side of this "generation gap" stood adults who were sick and tired of a nation of kids who seemed to be running wild. On the other were millions of rebellious young people out to change the world. Disgusted with a society they considered too rigid, controlling, and materialistic, the younger generation had rejected many of their parents' values and accepted rules of behavior. In place of that traditional American culture, they adopted their own alternative lifestyle—a "counterculture."

"Sex, drugs, and rock 'n' roll" was the rallying cry of the counterculture revolution. Young people experimented with freer sexual behavior and with mind-altering drugs such as marijuana and LSD. When parents and doctors warned about the very real dangers of using drugs, they laughed. After all, the older generation used drugs, too—cigarettes, alcohol, and a mountain of prescription sleeping pills and "pep" pills. Of course, not everyone—young or old—used drugs. But by 1971 more than half of all college-age students admitted that they had tried marijuana, or pot. And, observed college student David Obst, "If you smoked pot, and it was virtually [nearly] impossible not to if you were a college-age kid, then . . . you were part of the counterculture."

The lyrics of rock-and-roll songs often celebrated drug use. That was just one more reason for the older generation to disapprove of this revolutionary new music style. Born in the mid-1950s, rock had grown up to become the official music of youth. Political, religious, and business leaders condemned it. One New York radio disk jockey called rock "poor music, badly recorded, with lyrics that are at best in bad taste, and at worst obscene." The Reverend Billy Graham dismissed rock music as "a passing phase . . . the symptoms of the times and the confusion about us."

Besides their choice of music, there were lots of other ways for young people to assert their independence—and annoy their elders. Thumbing their noses at their parents' conservative

ROCK GUITARIST AND SUPERSTAR
JIMI HENDRIX

dress code, many youths sported torn blue jeans and ragged T-shirts, beaded headbands, "love beads," sandals or bare feet, and, especially, long shaggy hair. Those most deeply committed to the counterculture—the antiestablishment, pro-peace-and-love "hippies"—sometimes "dropped out" of traditional society to live in

Music of the Vietnam War

In the Vietnam War years—especially in the 1960s—rock and roll ruled. Many conservative adults were shocked by rock's earsplitting volume, throbbing beat, and references to sex and drugs. But to the younger generation, rock music touched a deep core of frustration, energy, rebellion . . . and it was great fun, too. Also hot during the 1960s and 1970s were folk music and the "Motown sound"—a distinctive blend of pop and soul music by African-American performers.

Top Rock Songs

"I Want to Hold Your Hand" (The Beatles)
"(I Can't Get No) Satisfaction"
(The Rolling Stones)
"Light My Fire" (The Doors)
"Somebody to Love" (Jefferson Airplane)
"We Gotta Get Out of This Place"
(The Animals)

Rock Antiwar Songs

"I-Feel-Like-I'm-Fixin'-To-Die Rag"
(Country Joe and the Fish)
"Fortunate Son"
(Creedence Clearwater Revival)
"Give Peace a Chance" (John Lennon)
"Ohio" (Crosby, Stills, Nash, and Young)

Motown Hits

"Stop! In the Name of Love"
(The Supremes)
"My Girl" (The Temptations)
"I Can't Help Myself (Sugar Pie, Honey Bunch)" (The Four Tops)
"I Heard It Through the Grapevine"
(Marvin Gaye)

Folk Protest Songs

"Blowin' in the Wind" (Bob Dylan)
"Turn! Turn! Turn!" (The Byrds)
"Alice's Restaurant" (Arlo Guthrie)
"Saigon Bride" (Joan Baez)

communes, where they worked the land, sharing their labor and their possessions. In April 1969 a group of hippies in Berkeley, California, worked together to turn an empty lot into a "People's Park"—a shaded garden where people could play, sing, eat, and sleep under the stars. That celebration of the counterculture lifestyle ended in what one reporter described as "guerrilla warfare" when police sent to reclaim the property battled a crowd of young people determined to defend "their" park.

Four months later New York's Catskill Mountain region became the scene of another, more peaceful demonstration of the power of the youth movement. The Woodstock festival, a three-day celebration of music, drugs, brotherhood, love, and joyous rebellion, drew a half million young people to a farm field in Bethel, New York. Many of the brightest stars of the rock world performed: Janis Joplin, Jimi Hendrix, the Who, the Grateful Dead, Jefferson Airplane, Santana. Festival-goers slept in blankets or sleeping bags, soaked by the rain, sharing their food and skinny-dipping in a nearby pond. "There was a feeling of community," remembers one man, "a spirit of cooperation that touched everyone. . . . It may have only existed for a few days, but it lives on in some form in all of us." Atlanta Lissiter of Phoenix, Arizona, declares that "Woodstock lives in my heart FOREVER! I will never forget the music, the people . . . the mud, the smell (it stunk!), and the peace and togetherness of us all!" To the *New York Times*, the festival was

> *a social phenomenon [rare event]. . . . And in spite of the prevalence [widespread use] of drugs it was essentially a phenomenon of innocence. . . . The police and the festival's promoters both expressed amazement that despite the size of the crowd—the largest gathering of its kind ever held—there had been neither violence nor any serious incident. . . . [People] came, it seems, to enjoy their own society, free to exult in a lifestyle that is its own declaration of independence.*

FOR THREE DAYS IN AUGUST 1969, A HALF MILLION YOUNG PEOPLE TURNED THE SITE OF THE WOODSTOCK FESTIVAL IN TINY BETHEL, NEW YORK, INTO THE STATE'S THIRD-LARGEST CITY.

"Hard Hats" and "Hairs"

Toward the end of 1969, more and more Americans, both young and old, were calling for the withdrawal of U.S. forces from Vietnam. President Nixon, however, was determined not to go down in history as "the first president of the United States to lose a war." Hoping to build support for his policies, the president asked the "great silent majority" of Americans to show their patriotism by denouncing the antiwar movement.

Millions of working-class Americans responded. Fed up with campus protests and the whole counterculture movement, they staged patriotic rallies and parades, waving American flags and banners bearing the slogan, "America—love it or leave it!" To keep the "silent majority" shouting, Nixon unleashed Vice President Spiro Agnew in a series of sharp attacks that labeled anyone who spoke out against the administration's policies as a dangerous "radical liberal." In one typically high-flying speech, Agnew called for

> *the preponderant [dominant] majority, the responsible citizens of this country, to assert* their *rights. It is time to stop dignifying the immature actions of an arrogant, reckless, inexperienced element within our society. The reason is compelling. It is simply that their tantrums are insidiously [sneakily] destroying the fabric of American democracy.*

Agnew's attacks helped whip up yet another division in American society— some called it "hard hats versus hairs." But even hard-hatted, hippie-hating construction workers were growing frustrated with the war. "It's people like us who give our sons for the country," explained a man who had lost his son in Vietnam. "I hate those peace demonstrators . . . [but] the sooner we get . . . out of there the better."

VICE PRESIDENT SPIRO AGNEW WAS A LOUD AND BITTER CRITIC OF WAR PROTESTERS—AND ANYONE ELSE WHO DISAGREED WITH GOVERNMENT POLICIES.

NOVEMBER 1969 BROUGHT NEWS THAT HORRIFIED AND SADDENED AMERICANS AND INCREASED SUPPORT FOR A SPEEDY END TO THE WAR. WORD HAD LEAKED OUT OF A BRUTAL MASSACRE OF SOUTH VIETNAMESE CIVILIANS BY AMERICAN TROOPS. MORE THAN A YEAR EARLIER, REPORTERS REVEALED, SOLDIERS SEARCHING FOR VIETCONG GUERRILLAS IN THE SOUTH VIETNAMESE VILLAGE OF MY LAI (PRONOUNCED ME-LIE) HAD SLAUGHTERED FIVE HUNDRED OLD MEN, WOMEN, AND CHILDREN. THE COMPANY'S COMMANDER, LIEUTENANT WILLIAM CALLEY, WOULD LATER BE TRIED FOR WAR CRIMES, SENTENCED TO LIFE IMPRISONMENT, AND THEN RELEASED AFTER THREE YEARS.

IN THIS LETTER ONE OF THE MEN IN CALLEY'S UNIT, WHO REFUSED TO TAKE PART IN THE KILLINGS, DESCRIBED AN INCIDENT THAT TOOK PLACE TWO DAYS BEFORE THE MY LAI MASSACRE. THE VIOLENCE WAS A SIGN OF THE ANGER AND FRUSTRATION GIs FELT AS THEY FOUGHT A WAR WITH NO FRONT LINES, AGAINST AN OFTEN "INVISIBLE" ENEMY—AN ENEMY THAT COULD INCLUDE GUERILLAS WAITING IN AMBUSH IN THE JUNGLE AND "FRIENDLY" VILLAGERS PLANTING BOOBY TRAPS.

[Thursday]
[March 14, 1968]

Dear Dad:

How's everything with you?

I'm still on the bridge, we leave here Saturday.

One of our platoons went out on a routine patrol today and came across a 155-mm artillery round that was booby trapped. It killed one man, blew the legs off two others, and injured two more.

And it all turned out a bad day made even worse. On their way back to [camp] they saw a woman working in the fields. They shot and wounded her. Then they kicked her to death and emptied their magazines [ammunition chambers] in her head. They slugged every little kid they came across.

Why in God's name does this have to happen? These are all seemingly normal guys; some were friends of mine. For a while they were like wild animals.

It was murder, and I'm ashamed of myself for not trying to do anything about it.

This isn't the first time, Dad. I've seen it many times before. I don't know why I'm telling you all this; I guess I just want to get it off my chest.

My faith in my fellow man is shot all to hell. I just want the time to pass and I just want to come home. . . .

Saturday we're going to be dropped by air in an N.V.A. [North Vietnamese Army] stronghold [My Lai]. . . .

I love and miss you and Mom so much—

Your son,
Greg

By the spring of 1971, polls showed that 51 percent of all Americans believed that the war in Vietnam was "morally wrong." That April some 750,000 people marched on Washington in the largest demonstration the nation had ever known. The protesters included vast crowds of hard-hatted union members—truckers, meat cutters, electrical workers, seamstresses—as well as members of the newly formed Vietnam Veterans Against the War. One middle-aged mother and her two children carried a banner reading, "The Majority Is Not Silent—The Government Is Deaf."

BY THE LATE 1960S, MANY AMERICAN VETERANS HAD ADDED THEIR VOICES TO THE ANTIWAR CAUSE.

Many of these new converts to the antiwar cause had simply come to the conclusion that the war was too costly. *Life* magazine had made the point movingly, with an issue that carried the photos of 242 young servicemen killed in one week in Vietnam. "A lot of us didn't speak out earlier," argued a "hard hat" at an antiwar rally, "and a lot of kids are dead because of it."

Death had also come to the homefront. As antiwar actions grew increasingly militant, police reaction became angrier and more violent. In 1969 students who had taken over a building at Harvard University were kicked and clubbed by police. Forty-one students and seven police officers ended up in the hospital. Then, in May 1970, the nation was shocked when National Guardsmen sent to restore order after demonstrations at Kent State University in Ohio opened fire on a crowd of students, killing four. Two weeks later

BLACK-SHROUDED DEMONSTRATORS MARCH IN PROTEST AGAINST THE KILLING OF FOUR STUDENTS BY NATIONAL GUARDSMEN AT KENT STATE UNIVERSITY.

two youngsters at Jackson State College in Mississippi were killed when police fired into a student dormitory after an antiwar protest.

Americans had another reason for rallying to the antiwar cause: the dawning suspicion that their leaders could no longer be trusted. In June 1971 the *New York Times* began publishing the Pentagon Papers, a collection of top secret government documents that had been stolen and released to the press by a former Defense Department employee, Daniel Ellsberg. The documents traced the history of U.S. involvement in Southeast Asia from 1945 through Lyndon Johnson's administration. They revealed the half-truths and lies used by U.S. presidents and military leaders to conceal questionable or illegal actions in Vietnam, to widen the war while promising to end it, and to convince the American public that victory was near when all evidence pointed to a long, uphill fight.

DEFENSE DEPARTMENT EMPLOYEE DANIEL ELLSBERG HELPED PREPARE THE TOP SECRET PENTAGON PAPERS, THEN "LEAKED" THEM TO THE PRESS AFTER HE BECAME CONVINCED U.S. POLICY-MAKERS HAD LIED TO THE PUBLIC.

President Nixon tried to stop publication of the Pentagon Papers. His efforts were overruled by the Supreme Court, but they fueled concerns that the government was still lying about Vietnam. Many Americans began to believe that what their leaders said was one thing, and what was really happening was another. This lack of faith in the truthfulness of government pronouncements became known as the credibility gap.

ANGERED OVER THE PUBLICATION OF THE PENTAGON PAPERS, PRESIDENT NIXON ORDERED AIDES TO FORM A SPECIAL WHITE HOUSE UNIT TO "PLUG" LEAKS OF GOVERNMENT SECRETS. JOKINGLY KNOWN AS THE "PLUMBERS," THE UNDERCOVER AGENTS CONDUCTED ILLEGAL ACTIVITIES TO GATHER INFORMATION ON THE PRESIDENT'S OPPONENTS. ON JUNE 17, 1972, THEY WERE CAUGHT BREAKING INTO DEMOCRATIC PARTY HEADQUARTERS AT THE WATERGATE BUILDING IN WASHINGTON TO BUG THE PHONES. THE PLUMBERS' CRIMES AND THE GOVERNMENT COVER-UP THAT FOLLOWED, KNOWN AS THE WATERGATE SCANDAL, LED TO PRESIDENT NIXON'S RESIGNATION IN 1974.

IN THIS CONVERSATION TAPED IN THE OVAL OFFICE SHORTLY AFTER THE WATERGATE BREAK-IN, THE PRESIDENT AND HIS CHIEF OF STAFF, H. R. HALDEMAN, WORRY THAT FBI (FEDERAL BUREAU OF INVESTIGATION) AGENTS MIGHT DISCOVER THAT MONEY ILLEGALLY DONATED TO THE NIXON REELECTION CAMPAIGN WAS USED TO FINANCE THE PLUMBERS' OPERATION. NIXON AGREES TO A PLAN TO HAVE THE CIA (CENTRAL INTELLIGENCE AGENCY) DISRUPT THE FBI'S INVESTIGATION. THIS RECORDING HAS BEEN CALLED THE "SMOKING GUN" TAPE, BECAUSE IT PROVIDED PROOF THAT THE PRESIDENT WAS INVOLVED IN THE COVER-UP FROM THE VERY BEGINNING.

HALDEMAN: Now, on the investigation, you know, the Democratic break-in thing, we're back in the problem area because the FBI is not under control, because [FBI Director Pat] Gray doesn't exactly know how to control them, and they have—their investigation is now leading into some productive areas, because they've been able to trace the money. . . . [Attorney General John] Mitchell came up with yesterday—and [presidential counsel] John Dean analyzed very carefully last night and [agrees] now with Mitchell's recommendation—that the only way to solve this . . . is for us to have [CIA Deputy Director Vernon] Walters call Pat Gray and just say, "Stay the hell out of this . . . this is, ah, business here, we don't want you to go any further on it." . . .

NIXON: What about Pat Gray, ah, you mean he doesn't want to?

HALDEMAN: Pat does want to. He doesn't know how to, and he doesn't have— he doesn't have any basis for doing it. Given this, he will then have the basis. . . .

NIXON: Good. Good deal! Play it tough. That's the way they play it and that's the way we are going to play it.

HALDEMAN: Okay. We'll do it. . . .

NIXON: When you get in these people [the CIA], when you . . . get these people in, say, "Look, . . . the President just feels that, ah"—without going into the details—don't, don't lie to them to the extent to say there is no involvement, but just say this is sort of a comedy of errors, bizarre, without getting into it, . . . that they should call the FBI in and say that we wish for the country, don't go any further into this case, period!

HALDEMAN: Okay.

NIXON: That's the way to put it, do it straight.

Back to "the World"

Antiwar pressures from all levels of American society finally forced President Nixon to begin troop withdrawals. By the end of 1971, about 157,000 servicemen and women remained in Vietnam— roughly half the number there a year earlier. Meanwhile, Nixon's national security adviser, Henry Kissinger, was holding secret talks with North Vietnam, seeking what the president called "peace with honor." In October 1972 Kissinger went on television to announce, "Peace is at hand. . . . We believe that an agreement is within sight." A month later Americans, relieved that the long war was finally coming to an end, reelected Nixon by a landslide over the Democratic candidate, George McGovern.

In early 1973 Kissinger and the North Vietnamese negotiators reached an agreement. The Paris Peace Accords, signed on January 27, called for a cease-fire, return of all American prisoners of war, and withdrawal of U.S. forces from Vietnam. North Vietnamese forces would be permitted to remain in South Vietnam while an international council was set up to plan elections and work toward permanent peace.

On March 29 the last American soldiers in Vietnam boarded planes and took off for what they called "the World." But for many Vietnam veterans, coming home was a shock. "I landed at Travis Air Force Base in California," recalls U.S. Army veteran Frank McCarthy.

> *I did the traditional things, kiss the ground when I got off the plane, and all that. I was so happy that I had survived. . . . As I'm riding down Telegraph Avenue [in Berkeley] I told the cab driver that I wanted to walk. . . . I was in my uniform. I was spit on. This gang of guys walking behind me threw peanuts at me. I went into a bar and phoned my brother. . . . The real shock of coming back was in that bar. These guys weren't going to let me out. They wanted to kick my ass. Calling, "You kill any women? You kill any kids?"*

Frank McCarthy's experience was not unusual. Veterans frequently encountered hostility or indifference from a nation eager to put the Vietnam War behind it. There were no victory parades like those held for veterans of earlier wars, no thanks for sacrifice and service. Some people seemed to think that all Vietnam veterans were like those who had taken part in the My Lai massacre. Others just wanted to forget the war and the men who fought it. "I felt my country didn't give a damn about me or the sacrifice I and thousands of others [had made] in their name," said veteran

David Donovan. To Patrick Gray of Nebraska, whose first greeting on U.S. soil came from a stranger hissing, "God-damned murderer," the answer was simple: "I guess guys who lose a war get pretty unpopular."

Lack of appreciation was just one of the problems Vietnam veterans faced. With the U.S. economy struggling to recover from the costs of war, jobs were hard to find, and veterans often seemed to be the last hired. Government benefits for education and job training were stingy compared with those provided after World War II. Medical care for wounded and disabled veterans was inadequate. Many veterans, especially those who had seen heavy combat, suffered from depression, nightmares, panic attacks, flashbacks of buried memories—all symptoms of a psychological illness called post-traumatic stress disorder. Some committed suicide; some became drug addicts or alcoholics. Many more fought a long uphill battle back into American society and built satisfying, productive lives.

A major step toward healing came in 1982, ten years after the war's end, with the opening of the Vietnam Veterans Memorial in Washington, D.C. During the dedication ceremonies, 150,000 veterans paraded through the streets of Washington. "Men, women, and children were cheering and waving flags," recalls David Donovan.

The most common cheer was "Welcome home! Welcome home!" . . . The tears kept filling my eyes, but this time not from sadness—it was from pleasure and immense relief. A parade! For me. A great weight was lifted from my shoulders. . . . I finally got my parade.

"I Have Never Forgotten You"

In 1982 the Vietnam Veterans Memorial was dedicated in Washington, D.C. Strikingly different from most other war monuments, with their statues and flags, the Vietnam memorial is a simple 492-foot-long wall made of panels of highly polished black granite. Carved into the surface of the stone are the names of the 58,195 servicemen and women killed or missing in Vietnam. Millions of people visit the Wall each year. Many leave behind letters, poems, photographs, and other personal remembrances in honor of a friend or loved one who went to Vietnam and never came back.

I am the one who rocked him as a baby. I am the one who kissed away the hurts. I'm the one who taught him right from wrong. I'm the one who held him for the last time and watched him fly away to war. I'm the one who prayed each night "Dear God keep him safe." I'm the goofy mom who sent him a Christmas tree in Vietnam. I'm the one whose heart broke when told my Billy had died in a helicopter crash. And now I'm the one who still cries at night because of all the memories I have that will never die.

Oh, yes, Billy, this mother of yours remembers. I remember the good times and I remember the bad times. But you were so full of life and kept me busy the 21 years I had you, that I now thank God for letting me be your Mom and for leaving me so many more good memories than bad ones. I love you, Billy, and I miss you so.

Mom

To: Michael "Bat" Masterson
Well here you are, making another lasting impression on me and everyone else who sees you! I love you so much. I have dreamed of the day you'll come home and finally be my Dad. You would have been the best Daddy in the whole world. You were for the short period of time in my life. I can never forget you. I'm 23 now! I sure look a lot different from six years old. You'd be very proud of me. They say I'm a lot like you. I can see it too. I have never forgotten you. I knew you were Santa Claus, but I didn't want to spoil it for you.

Your daughter,
Sheri

Before he left, he taught me how to drive his car. Then he left it to me to take care of it "'til he got back."

"Dad survived Iwo Jima, Guadalcanal and all that. I'm a Marine. I'll be back. Take care of my car."

I've still got the car. I would rather have my big brother back.

THE VIETNAM VETERANS MEMORIAL HAS BECOME ONE OF THE MOST VISITED SITES IN WASHINGTON, D.C.—A PLACE FOR REMEMBERING, GRIEVING, AND HONORING THOSE WHO SERVED.

CONCLUSION: LOSSES AND LESSONS

America's longest and most unpopular war took the lives of more than 58,000 servicemen and women. Another 300,000 were wounded, many disabled for life. About 2,000 GIs are listed as missing in action (MIA). Thirty years later their families, still clinging to hopes that a loved one is alive and imprisoned in Vietnam, press the government to work harder investigating their cases. For these people—and for the thousands of veterans suffering from lasting psychological harm or from health problems stemming from exposure to Agent Orange, a chemical used to destroy vegetation in Vietnam—the war is not over yet.

The end of U.S. involvement did not bring peace for the people of Vietnam, either. With the ink barely dry on the Paris Peace Accords, both North and South Vietnam began to violate the truce. Without U.S. backing, the south didn't stand a chance. On April 30, 1975—two years after the withdrawal of American troops—North Vietnamese Army tanks rumbled into the southern capital at Saigon and proclaimed the country "reunited" under Communist rule. An estimated two million Vietnamese, north and south, soldier and civilian, had died since the arrival of the first

CASKETS BEARING THE BODIES OF U.S. SERVICEMEN
KILLED IN VIETNAM RETURN HOME.

U.S. combat troops in 1965. In the years following the war, millions more struggled to recover from the devastating poverty and destruction the conflict left behind. Today that situation is changing. Although most Vietnamese are still poor, relaxed government policies and renewed trade with the world's free nations have brought a growing economy and hopes of a brighter future.

U.S. involvement in Vietnam—and the antiwar movement and other social causes inspired by it—also brought lasting change to the American homefront. Many young people who had become politically active during the war years continued to work for a better society, through careers in politics or volunteer work in their local communities. Many universities revised their policies in response to student demands, admitting more minority students, adding courses on black and women's studies, and relaxing rules that limited students' freedoms. American society as a whole became more open to differences in dress and lifestyle: long hair for men, slacks for women, couples living together without marriage. Out of the feminist revolution came real progress toward equal rights for women, while the civil rights movement swept Africans Americans into voting booths and black leaders into political office.

Just as dramatic were the changes in the way Americans see their nation and their government. Vietnam was the first war the United States lost. It shattered the widespread conviction that the U.S. was so powerful it could defeat any enemy and achieve any goal. Gone, too, was the American people's blind faith in the honesty of their elected officials. The deceptions practiced during the war and the Watergate scandal that followed on its heels created a credibility gap—a doubt and mistrust of government—that has never been fully overcome.

Today Americans are wary of sending their armed forces to fight in foreign conflicts unless the cause is clear—an attitude known as the "Vietnam syndrome." This reluctance to wage war

IN AUGUST 1974, FACED WITH THE THREAT OF BEING REMOVED FROM OFFICE FOR HIS
ROLE IN THE WATERGATE SCANDAL, RICHARD NIXON BECAME THE FIRST U.S.
PRESIDENT EVER TO RESIGN.

without a full and careful debate, reinforced by the knowledge
that there are limits to U.S. power, may be one of the war's few
happy outcomes. By learning the lessons of Vietnam, Americans
may finally heal the nation's wounds and ensure that the same
mistakes are never made again.

THE VIETNAM WAR YEARS— TIME LINE OF EVENTS

June 19
Congress passes the Civil Rights Act, banning discrimination in public facilities, education, and employment.

August 7
Congress passes the Gulf of Tonkin Resolution, giving the president unlimited power to resist aggression in Southeast Asia.

November 3
Lyndon Johnson is elected president.

February 12
The U.S. sends advisers to train the South Vietnamese army.

October 26
U.S.-backed Ngo Dinh Diem becomes president of South Vietnam.

November 8
John F. Kennedy is elected 35th president of the United States.

October 29
NOW (the National Organization for Women) is founded.

1954 1955 1959 1960 1963 1964 1965 1966

May 7
Ho Chi Minh's Vietnamese Communists defeat the French at Dien Bien Phu.

May 17
The U.S. Supreme Court rules in the Brown v. Board of Education case, holding that segregation in public schools violates the Constitution.

July 21
The Geneva Conference calls for a cease-fire in Vietnam and divides the country, with Ho Chi Minh leading in the north and Bao Dai in the south.

July 8
Two U.S. military advisers die in a Vietcong attack— the first Americans killed in the Vietnam War.

February
Betty Friedan's *The Feminine Mystique* is published.

November 1
A U.S.-backed military coup overthrows the Diem government.

November 22
President Kennedy is assassinated; Vice President Lyndon Johnson becomes president.

March 2
The U.S. Air Force begins Rolling Thunder bombing campaign in North Vietnam.

March 8
3,500 U.S. Marines land at Da Nang— the first American combat troops in Vietnam.

April 17
The first major antiwar demonstration takes place in Washington, D.C.

April 15
In New York and San Francisco, more than 200,000 demonstrate against the war.

October 21
50,000 antiwar protesters march on the Pentagon.

June 8
Nixon announces the first U.S. troop withdrawals from Vietnam.

August 15–18
The Woodstock music festival is held in Bethel, New York.

April 24
750,000 antiwar protesters participate in the March on Washington— the largest demonstration in U.S. history.

June 13
The *New York Times* begins publishing the Pentagon Papers, the Defense Department's secret report on U.S. involvement in Vietnam.

January 27
The U.S., North Vietnam, South Vietnam, and the Vietcong sign the Paris Peace Accords, agreeing to a cease-fire and withdrawal of all U.S. troops from Vietnam.

March 29
The last U.S. combat troops leave Vietnam.

January 8
North Vietnamese forces begin a major offensive against South Vietnam.

April 30
Saigon surrenders to North Vietnam. Remaining U.S. personnel and selected South Vietnamese are evacuated from the roof of the U.S. Embassy.

| 1967 | 1968 | 1969 | 1970 | 1971 | 1972 | 1973 | 1974 | 1975 |

January 31
North Vietnam launches the Tet Offensive, a massive surprise attack on cities and military bases throughout South Vietnam.

March 16
U.S. soldiers massacre Vietnamese civilians at My Lai.

March 31
President Johnson announces that he will not seek a second term.

April 4
Civil rights leader Dr. Martin Luther King, Jr., is assassinated.

June 5
Presidential candidate Robert Kennedy is assassinated.

August 25–29
Antiwar protests, rioting, and police violence disrupt the Democratic National Convention in Chicago.

November 5
Richard Nixon is elected president of the United States.

February 20
National security adviser Henry Kissinger begins secret peace talks with North Vietnam's Le Duc Tho in Paris.

April 29
U.S. troops invade Cambodia to attack North Vietnamese and Vietcong sanctuaries.

May 4
Four students are killed by Ohio National Guardsmen at Kent State University.

June 17
Five men are caught breaking into Democratic Party headquarters at Washington's Watergate complex to install bugging equipment for the Nixon reelection campaign.

November 7
Richard Nixon is reelected president.

August 9
Nixon resigns to avoid impeachment for his role in the Watergate scandal; Vice President Gerald Ford becomes president.

GLOSSARY

baby boom The sharp increase in the U.S. birthrate that followed World War II, resulting mostly from an increase in marriages and prosperity; people born during this time are known as "baby boomers."

boycott To refuse to buy from or deal with a business, usually as a form of protest.

cold war The period between the end of World War II and the collapse of the Soviet Union in the early 1990s, marked by hostility between the democratic nations of the West and the Soviet Union and other Communist nations.

Communism A system in which all property is owned and controlled by the government and is supposed to be shared equally by all citizens.

counterculture A culture with values and rules of behavior different from traditional society.

credibility gap A lack of confidence in the truthfulness of government statements.

domino theory An idea often used to justify U.S. intervention in Vietnam, this theory stated that if one of the nations of Southeast Asia fell to Communist power, the rest would topple like a row of dominoes. Debate over the theory still continues: after the Vietnam War, Cambodia and Laos were taken over by the Communists but the other "dominoes" did not fall; supporters of the theory argue that this was because the U.S. involvement gave those nations time to strengthen their defenses against aggression.

feminist Someone who works in support of women's rights.

generation gap A wide difference in values and attitudes between younger and older generations.

ghetto A part of a city in which members of a minority group live, usually because of poverty and discrimination.

GI A member of the U.S. armed forces; the name comes from the servicemen's "government issue" supplies.

guerrilla (pronounced like "gorilla") A type of fighting or fighter that uses surprise and stealth instead of direct combat to wear down a better-equipped enemy.

integration The act of making schools and other public places and services open to people of all races; the ending of segregation.

materialistic Focused on possessions rather than things of the heart, mind, and spirit.

moderate A person who favors calm, reasonable viewpoints and actions.

Peace Corps A U.S. agency established by President John F. Kennedy in 1961, which sends volunteers to developing nations to help their citizens learn new skills to better their lives.

radical A person who favors extreme viewpoints and actions, which are intended to bring about extreme changes in government and society.

segregation The practice of separating one race or ethnic group from another by setting up separate housing, schools, and public facilities and through other forms of discrimination.

Vietcong South Vietnamese who supported and fought for the Communists.

TO FIND OUT MORE

Books and Periodicals

Brown, Gene. *The Nation in Turmoil: Civil Rights and the Vietnam War (1960–1973)*. First Person America series. New York: Henry Holt, 1993.
Examines the Vietnam War through excerpts from letters, diaries, songs, speeches, poems, and other writings of the era.

Burby, Liza N. *The Watts Riot*. World History series. San Diego: Lucent Books, 1997.
An informative account of the Watts riot of 1965, with a look at race relations and conditions in the inner cities today.

DeVaney, John. *The Vietnam War*. New York: Franklin Watts, 1992.
Easy-to-read account of the Vietnam War and homefront protests, with many dramatic stories told by people involved in the fighting.

Gay, Kathlyn, and Martin Gay. *Vietnam War*. Voices from the Past series. New York: Twenty-First Century Books, 1996.
This series brings a personal view to war, by weaving in accounts by the men and women who served in the armed forces as well as ordinary Americans on the homefront.

McCloud, Bill. *What Should We Tell Our Children about Vietnam?* Norman, OK: University of Oklahoma Press, 1989.
A collection of impressions and remembrances of the war by veterans, families of GIs killed or missing in action, and well-known writers and political leaders.

Marrin, Albert. *America and Vietnam: The Elephant and the Tiger*. New York: Viking, 1992.
Evenhanded discussion of the background and history of America's involvement in Vietnam and the American antiwar movement.

Stearman, Kaye. *Women's Rights: Changing Attitudes 1900–2000*. Austin, TX: Raintree Steck-Vaughn, 2000.
Examines women's status around the world and the history of the women's liberation movement, from the 1960s to the present day.

On the Internet*

"History and Politics Out Loud." ©1999–2000 Jerry Goldman and
    Northwestern University, at http://www.hpol.org
*Listen to private conversations and speeches by historical figures including
    John F. Kennedy, Robert Kennedy, Lyndon Johnson, Richard Nixon, and
    Martin Luther King. The site includes typed transcripts of the recordings.*

"Malcolm X: A Research Site," Africana Studies Program, University of
    Toledo, at http://www.brothermalcom.net
*Explores the life of radical black leader Malcolm X, and includes a detailed
    chronology of his activities, plus a review of his writings and speeches,
    including some with audio clips.*

"National Civil Rights Museum" at http://www.mecca.org/~crights
*This official website of the National Civil Rights Museum in Memphis,
    Tennessee, offers a virtual tour in words and photos. Includes informa-
    tion on slavery, the Civil War, segregation, and the civil rights movement.*

"Vietnam Then & Now" at http://library.thinkquest.org/25734
*This award-winning site for students includes information about the people,
    culture, and government of Vietnam today, as well as sections on
    Vietnamese history and the Vietnam War.*

*Websites change from time to time. For additional on-line information, check with
    the media specialist at your local library.

Video

Vietnam: A Television History. Written by Andrew Pearson. Produced by
    WGBH Educational Foundation, Boston, 1983. Distributed by
    Sony Video Software Company.
*This seven-volume video series won six Emmy Awards for its detailed visual
    and oral accounts of the history, costs, and consequences of the Vietnam
    War. Contains some graphic images and descriptions of war's violence.*

BIBLIOGRAPHY

Allen, Thomas B., ed. *Offerings at the Wall: Artifacts from the Vietnam Veterans Memorial Collection*. Atlanta: Turner Publishing, 1995.

"The American Experience: Vietnam Online." Produced for PBS Online by WGBH. ©1983, 1997 WGBH Educational Foundation. At http://www.pbs.org/wgbh/amex/vietnam

Archer, Jules. *The Incredible Sixties: The Stormy Years That Changed America*. San Diego: Harcourt Brace Jovanovich, 1986.

Beesley, Stanley W. *Vietnam: The Heartland Remembers*. Norman, OK: University of Oklahoma Press, 1987.

Boettcher, Thomas D. *Vietnam: The Valor and the Sorrow*. Boston: Little, Brown, 1985.

Capps, Walter H. *The Unfinished War: Vietnam and the American Conscience*. Boston: Beacon Press, 1982.

Caputo, Philip. *A Rumor of War*. New York: Ballantine Books, 1977.

Davis, Flora. *Moving the Mountain: The Women's Movement in America since 1960*. New York: Simon & Schuster, 1991.

Denenberg, Barry. *Voices from Vietnam*. New York: Scholastic, 1995.

Dougan, Clark, Samuel Lipsman, and the editors of Boston Publishing Company. *A Nation Divided*. Boston: Boston Publishing, 1984.

Dudley, William, and David Bender, eds. *The Vietnam War: Opposing Viewpoints*. San Diego: Greenhaven Press, 1990.

Dworkin, Susan. Edited by Suzanne Braun Levine. *She's Nobody's Baby: A History of American Women in the 20th Century*. New York: Simon & Schuster, 1983.

Edelman, Bernard, ed. *Dear America: Letters Home from Vietnam*. New York: Pocket Books, 1985.

Editorial Reports on the Women's Movement: Achievements and Effects. Washington, D.C.: Congressional Quarterly, 1977.

Farrell, Amy Erdman. *Yours in Sisterhood: Ms. Magazine and the Promise of Popular Feminism*. Chapel Hill, NC: University of North Carolina Press, 1998.

Fornatale, Pete. *The Story of Rock 'n' Roll*. New York: William Morrow, 1987.

Friedan, Betty. *The Feminine Mystique*. New York: W. W. Norton, 1974.

———. *It Changed My Life: Writings on the Women's Movement*. New York: Random House, 1976.

Garfinkle, Adam. *Telltale Hearts: The Origins and Impact of the Vietnam War Antiwar Movement*. New York: St. Martin's, 1995.

Goff, Stanley, Robert Sanders, and Clark Smith. *Brothers: Black Soldiers in the Nam*. Novato, CA: Presidio Press, 1982.

Hardy, Gordon, and the editors of Boston Publishing Company. *Words of War: An Anthology of Vietnam War Literature*. Boston: Boston Publishing Company, 1988.

Heineman, Kenneth J. *Campus Wars: The Peace Movement at American State Universities in the Vietnam Era*. New York: New York University Press, 1993.

Hoobler, Dorothy, and Thomas Hoobler. *Vietnam: Why We Fought*. New York: Alfred A. Knopf, 1990.

Karnow, Stanley. *Vietnam: A History*. New York: Viking, 1983.

King, Martin Luther, Jr. *Why We Can't Wait*. New York: Penguin, 1964.

Mahony, Phillip, ed. *From Both Sides Now: The Poetry of the Vietnam War and Its Aftermath*. New York: Scribner, 1998.

Morgan, Robin, ed. *Sisterhood Is Powerful: An Anthology of Writings from the Women's Liberation Movement*. New York: Random House, 1970.

Obst, David. *Too Good To Be Forgotten: Changing America in the '60s and '70s*. New York: John Wiley, 1998.

O'Nan, Stewart, ed. *The Vietnam Reader*. New York: Doubleday, 1998.

Palmer, Laura. *Shrapnel in the Heart: Letters and Remembrances from the Vietnam Veterans Memorial*. New York: Random House, 1987.

Pratt, John Clark, comp. *Vietnam Voices: Perspectives on the War Years, 1941–1982*. New York: Viking Penguin, 1984.

Rowe, John Carlos, and Rick Berg. *The Vietnam War and American Culture*. New York: Columbia University Press, 1991.

Santoli, Al. *To Bear Any Burden: The Vietnam War and Its Aftermath in the Words of Americans and Southeast Asians*. New York: Dutton, 1985.

Summers, Harry G., Jr. *Vietnam War Almanac*. New York: Facts on File, 1985.

Terry, Wallace. *Bloods: An Oral History of the Vietnam War by Black Veterans*. New York: Random House, 1984.

Whitney, Sharon. *The Equal Rights Amendment: The History and the Movement*. New York: Franklin Watts, 1984.

Wittman, Sandra M. "Vietnam Yesterday and Today" at http://server-cc.oakton.edu/~wittman

"Women Arise." *Life*, September 4, 1970.

Woodward, Bob, and Carl Bernstein. *The Final Days*. New York: Simon & Schuster, 1976.

Wright, David. *Causes and Consequences of the Vietnam War*. Austin, TX: Raintree Steck-Vaughn, 1996.

NOTES ON QUOTES

The quotations in this book are from the following sources:

Chapter One: The "Cold War" Heats Up

p. 12, "The idealism of JFK": Obst, *Too Good To Be Forgotten*, p. 55.

p. 12, "assure a more fruitful": John F. Kennedy inaugural address, January 20, 1961, from *History and Politics Out Loud*, ©1999–2000 Jerry Goldman and Northwestern University,
at http://database.library.northwestern.edu/hpol/transcript.asp?id=10

p. 13, "Let the word go forth": ibid.

p. 14, "wait for the nuclear" and "passionately anticommunist": Obst, *Too Good To Be Forgotten*, pp. 13, 54.

p. 14, "a row of dominoes": Denenberg, *Voices from Vietnam*, p. 5.

p. 14, "and Vietnam looks": Boettcher, *Vietnam*, p. 174.

p. 17, "I was relieved": Beesley, *Vietnam*, p. 5.

p. 17, "missionary idealism": Caputo, *Rumor of War*, p. xiv.

p. 19, "that nagging": Dougan and others, *Nation Divided*, p. 58.

p. 19, "take all necessary": Hoobler and Hoobler, *Why We Fought*, p. 72.

p. 19, "grandma's nightshirt": Karnow, *Vietnam*, p. 374.

p. 19, "I feel like": ibid., p. 396.

p. 21, "We kept": Caputo, *Rumor of War*, p. xiv.

Chapter Two: The War at Home

p. 22, "The weakest chink": Karnow, *Vietnam*, p. 481.

p. 22, "send American boys": Obst, *Too Good to Be Forgotten*, p. 63.

p. 24, "The majority": *Brown Alumni Monthly*, Providence, Rhode Island, October 1968, p. 29.

p. 25, "lesson in courage" and "young white men": *Civil Rights in Mississippi Digital Archive*, McCain Library & Archives, University of Southern Mississippi, at http://www.lib.usm.edu/~spcol/crda/oh/clemson.htm

p. 25, "The society": Gay and Gay, *Vietnam War*, p. 35.

p. 26, "Mom, I appreciate": Edelman, *Dear America*, p. 211.

p. 26, "The soldiers got": *Vietnam*, Episode 5: *America Takes Charge*.

p. 26, "A lot of people": Dennis Hodo e-mail to author, October 7, 1999.

p. 26, "You can't understand": Edelman, *Dear America*, p. 211.

p. 30, "The promises": Denenberg, *Voices from Vietnam*, p. 105.

p. 30, "bearded leftist brats": *West Essex Tribune*, Livingston, NJ, May 22, 1969, p. 15.

p. 33, "taking place": Karnow, *Vietnam*, p. 479.

p. 35, "I shall not seek": Denenberg, *Voices from Vietnam*, p. 148.

p. 37, "out for social": Dougan and others, *Nation Divided*, p. 106.

p. 37, "You are quite right": Avorn, *Up Against the Ivy Wall*, pp. 26-27.

p. 39, "a pack of wolves": Obst, *Too Good To Be Forgotten*, p. 111.

Chapter Three: The Civil Rights Movement

p. 40, 41, "I remember once" and "For instance": *Civil Rights in Mississippi Digital Archive*, at http://lib.usm.edu/~spcol/crda/oh/baker.htm

p. 41, "no different": Terry, *Bloods*, p. 136.

p. 42, "the stinging darts": King, *Why We Can't Wait*, p. 81.

p. 45, "I have a dream": *Martin Luther King, Jr., Papers Project at Stanford University*, at http://www.stanford.edu/group/King

p. 46, "an immediate end": *The Black Panther Party* at http://www.cs.oberlin.edu/students/pjaques/etext/bpp_program.html

p. 46, "We must move": Archer, *Incredible Sixties*, p. 37.

p. 48, "You could go": Terry, *Bloods*, p. 191.

p. 48, "that they put us": Goff and others, *Brothers*, p. 132.

p. 48, "just wanted": ibid., p. 133.

p. 48, "paid a special": Terry, *Bloods*, p. 205.

p. 51, "Why should": ibid., p. 116.

p. 51, "kick whitey's ass": ibid., pp. 14–15.

p. 51, "We are part": ibid., p. 116.

Chapter Four: "Women Arise"

p. 52, "Women have accepted": "Women Arise," p. 21.

p. 52, *"remember the ladies"*: Whitney, *Equal Rights Amendment*, p. 3.

p. 52, "Women made peanut butter": Dworkin, *She's Nobody's Baby*, p. 162.

p. 53, "Licking stamps" and "Power to": Archer, *Incredible Sixties*, p. 126.

p. 53, "a deep sense": Friedan, *Feminine Mystique*, p. 229.

p. 54, "In the magazine": ibid., p. 36.

p. 55, "In 36 states": "Women Arise," pp. 18–19.

p. 55, "a leading role": Morgan, *Sisterhood Is Powerful*, p. 443.

p. 57, "I did not set": Friedan, *It Changed My Life*, p. xiii.

p. 58, "a new movement": ibid., p. 87.

p. 58, "revolution that": "Women Arise," p. 16B.

p. 59, "For the life": "Letters to the Editor," *Life*, September 25, 1970, p. 25.

p. 59, "sick of having": Friedan, *It Changed My Life*, p. 23.

p. 59, "distorted minds": Whitney, *Equal Rights Amendment*, p. 65.

p. 59, "a total assault": Farrell, *Yours in Sisterhood*, p. 51.

p. 59, "Not by": Friedan, *It Changed My Life*, p. 369.

p. 59, "There could be": Davis, *Moving the Mountain*, p. 492.

Chapter Five: A Bitter Peace

p. 62, "Tin soldiers": "Ohio," written by Neil Young, performed by Crosby, Stills, Nash, and Young, *4 Way Street* album, Atlantic Recording Corp., 1971.

p. 62, "sex, drugs": Dougan and others, *Nation Divided*, p. 138.

p. 63, "If you smoked": Obst, *Too Good To Be Forgotten*, p. 200.

p. 63, "poor music": Fornatale, *Rock 'n' Roll*, p. 7.

p. 63, "a passing phase": *The Birth of Rock and Roll*, at http://www.about.com/musicperform/classicrock/library/weekly/aa022598.htm

p. 65, "guerrilla warfare": Dougan and others, *Nation Divided*, p. 162.

p. 65, "There was a feeling" and "Woodstock lives": *1969 Woodstock Festival & Concert,* at http://www.woodstock69.com/woodstock_mem.htm

p. 65, "a social phenomenon": Dougan and others, *Nation Divided,* p. 166.

p. 66, "the first president": Karnow, *Vietnam,* p. 577.

p. 67, "great silent majority": ibid., p. 600.

p. 67, "the preponderant": Hardy and others, *Words of War,* p. 167.

p. 67, "It's people": Dougan and others, *Nation Divided,* p. 157.

p. 69, "morally wrong": Karnow, *Vietnam,* p. 632.

p. 69, "The Majority Is": Dougan and others, *Nation Divided,* p. 177.

p. 70, "A lot of us": ibid.

p. 73, "peace with honor": Karnow, *Vietnam,* p. 654.

p. 73, "Peace is at hand": ibid., p. 651.

p. 74, "I landed": Santoli, *To Bear Any Burden,* p. 111.

p. 74, "I felt my country": Hoobler and Hoobler, *Why We Fought,* p. 183.

p. 75, "God-damned murderer": Gay and Gay, *Vietnam War,* p. 57.

p. 75, "Men, women, and children": Hoobler and Hoobler, *Why We Fought,* p. 184.

INDEX

Page numbers for illustrations are in **boldface**

ABOUT THE AUTHOR

"The hours I spent at libraries searching for the 'voices' of the LETTERS FROM THE HOME-FRONT series were filled with delightful discoveries: crayon notes from a kindergartner to his big brother serving in Vietnam, a cardboard box crammed with more than a thousand letters sent to a World War II serviceman in Europe by his devoted fiancée, golden locks of hair tucked inside the crumbling leather diary kept by a Pennsylvania woman during the Civil War. What struck me most was how familiar all these voices sounded. In times of trouble, it seems, people through the centuries have shared much the same doubts and fears, bitterness and heartache, love of family and country, humor, courage, dreams. I hope readers will be touched by the same sense of discovery and appreciation of the indomitable American spirit."

VIRGINIA SCHOMP has written dozens of books for young readers, including many published by Marshall Cavendish on subjects ranging from history to biography to careers. Ms. Schomp lives in New York's Catskill Mountains with her husband (and A-1 research assistant), Richard, and their son (and champion reader), Chip.